W9-BBT-575

ALSO BY NEIL POSTMAN

The End of Education

Technopoly

Conscientious Objections

Teaching as a Subversive Activity
(WITH CHARLES WEINGARTNER)

Crazy Talk, Stupid Talk

Teaching as a Conserving Activity

The Disappearance of Childhood

Amusing Ourselves to Death

Building a Bridge
to the 18th Century

Building a Bridge to the 18th Century

How the Past Can Improve Our Future

Neil Postman

 Alfred A. Knopf   New York   2000

THIS IS A BORZOI BOOK
PUBLISHED BY ALFRED A. KNOPF, INC.

Copyright © 1999 by Neil Postman

All rights reserved under International and Pan-American
Copyright Conventions. Published in the United States by
Alfred A. Knopf, Inc., New York, and simultaneously in
Canada by Random House of Canada Limited, Toronto.
Distributed by Random House, Inc., New York.

www.randomhouse.com

Knopf, Borzoi Books, and the colophon are registered
trademarks of Random House, Inc.

Grateful acknowledgment is made to the following for permis-
sion to reprint previously published material: *Edna St.
Vincent Millay Society:* Excerpt from "Upon this age, that never speaks
its mind" by Edna St. Vincent Millay, from *Collected Poems* by
Edna St. Vincent Millay (New York, HarperCollins), copyright
© 1939, 1967 by Edna St. Vincent Millay and Norma Millay
Ellis. All rights reserved. Reprinted by permission of Elizabeth
Barnett, Literary Executor, Edna St. Vincent Millay Society.
Houghton Mifflin Company: Excerpt of February 25, 1812, letter
from Lord Byron to Lord Holland, from *Lord Byron: Selected
Poems and Letters,* edited by William H. Marshall (Riverside
Edition), copyright © 1968 by Houghton Mifflin Company.
Reprinted courtesy of Houghton Mifflin Company.

Library of Congress Cataloging-in Publication Data
Postman, Neil.
Building a bridge to the 18th century: how the past
can improve our future / by Neil Postman.—1st ed.
p.   cm.
Includes bibliographical references and index.
ISBN 0-375-40129-6 (alk. paper)
1. Civilization, Modern—1950– 2. United States—Civilization—1970– 3. Enlightenment. 4. Technology and civilization. 5. Education—Philosophy. 6. Democracy. I. Title.
CB430.P637   1999
909.82'5—dc21   99-18923
                                                        CIP

Manufactured in the United States of America
Published October 6, 1999
Reprinted Once
Third Printing, February 2000

To Norman Frederick Ross

Soon we shall know everything the 18th century didn't know, and nothing it did, and it will be hard to live with us.

—RANDALL JARRELL

Contents

Building a Bridge
to the 18th Century

Author's Note

In this book, I have, inevitably, touched on themes that have interested me for thirty years. Thus, in a few places, when paraphrasing failed me, I have used passages that have appeared in earlier books. The context here is different from their original use but they seemed to fit, and I gave myself permission to use them. In all cases, of course, they are, for good or ill, my ideas and my words. The passages from previous writings of mine appear on pages 39, 64, 84, 85, 114, 115, 130, and 131. The first part of the chapter titled "Childhood" is a reprise of material used in *The Disappearance of Childhood*.

Prelude

Enlightenment (en·lit'n·ment) *n.* 1. A philosophical movement of the eighteenth century focusing on the criticism of previously accepted doctrines and institutions from the point of view of rationalism.

Enlightenment (en·lit'n·ment) *n.* 2. In April 1735, John Peter Zenger, the publisher of the *New York Weekly Journal,* was brought to trial on a charge of criminal libel. He was accused of having written that the liberties and property of the people of New York were threatened. It was charged against him that he said "men's deeds [were] destroyed, judges arbitrarily displaced, new courts erected without the consent of the legislature." At the time of the trial, no distinction in law was made, so far as "libel" was concerned, between true statements and false statements. The presiding Chief Justice noted that "You cannot be admitted . . . to give the truth of a libel in evidence. A libel is not to be justified; for it is nevertheless a libel that it is true."

Although Zenger admitted that he had published these statements, he nonetheless pleaded not guilty. On the basis of Zenger's admission, the chief prosecutor insisted that the jury must find a verdict for the King. He added that the fact that these words were true made the crime worse. The Chief Justice was inclined to agree with the prosecution. But Zenger's lawyer, Andrew Hamilton of Philadelphia, asked to be allowed to make his case before the jury. Here is an excerpt of what Hamilton said:

3

Prelude

I thank Your Honor. Then, gentlemen of the jury, it is to you we must now appeal, for witnesses to the truth of the facts we have offered, and are denied the liberty to prove; and let it not seem strange that I apply myself to you in this manner. I am warranted so to do both by law and reason. The last supposes you to be summoned *out of the neighborhood where the fact is alleged to be committed;* and the reason of your being taken out of the neighborhood is *because you are supposed to have the best knowledge of the fact that is to be tried.* And were you to find a verdict against my client, you must take upon you to say the papers referred to in the information, and which we acknowledge we printed and published, are *false, scandalous, and seditious;* but of this I can have no apprehension. You are citizens of New York; you are really what the law supposes you to be, *honest and lawful men;* and, according to my brief, the facts which we offer to prove were not committed in a corner; *they are notoriously known to be true;* and therefore in your justice lies our safety. . . .

It is true in times past it was a crime to speak truth, and in that terrible Court of Star Chamber many worthy and brave men suffered for so doing; and yet even in that court, and in those bad times, a great and good man durst say, what I hope will not be taken amiss of me to say in this place, *to wit, the practice of informations for libels is a sword in the hands of a wicked king.* . . .

When he was done, the jury retired. But they shortly returned, and, upon being asked if John Peter Zenger was guilty of printing and publishing libels, their foreman, Thomas Hunt, replied, "Not guilty."

Fifty-six years later the Bill of Rights was added to the American Constitution.

Introduction

The future is, of course, an illusion. Nothing has happened there yet. What Gertrude Stein said of Oakland, California, we may say of the future: There is no *there* there. Among Marshall McLuhan's many intriguing metaphors, the most paradoxical one is his reference to "rearview mirror" thinking. All of us, he said, are speeding along a highway with our eyes fixed on the rearview mirror, which can tell us only where we have been, not what lies ahead. He believed that only a few avant-garde artists (and, of course, himself) were capable of looking through the windshield so that they might tell us where we are going. The irony here is that the windshield is also a rearview mirror of sorts, for whatever future we see is only—can only be—a projection of the past.

In his journal, Søren Kierkegaard remarks that foresight is really hindsight, a reflection of the future revealed to the eye when it looks back upon the past. He implies that we are never free of the past, and those who read science fiction and other visionary tales will agree. Read *The Road Ahead* by Bill Gates, and you will see it is more history than prophecy, or perhaps we might say it is history as prophecy. Imagined futures are always more about where we have been than where we are going.

What, then, are we to make of George Santayana's famous aphorism, the one that tells us that if we forget the past we are condemned to relive it? Can we ever forget the past? Is it possible to plan a future, or even think about it, without reference to the past?

This book proceeds on the assumption that both Kierkegaard and Santayana are right. Kierkegaard is right in suggesting that there is nothing to see in the future except something from the past, and he invites us to be quite careful about what part of the past we use in imagining the future. And so does Santayana. Yes, he is urging us to remember our mistakes so that we do not repeat them. But he wants us to remember, as well, our glories. To forget our mistakes is bad. But to forget our successes may be worse.

In remembering the past, we must keep in mind that, while it is no illusion, it is elusive, a collection of shadowed memories immersed in ambiguities, wish fulfillments, and oversimplifications. Nonetheless, there is something there to see, to learn from, to provide material for new myths. There *is* a there there, and it will show itself through the windshield if we look hard enough in the rearview mirror.

Chapter One

A Bridge to the 18th Century

The day before I began writing this book, I heard on the radio that somewhere between thirty-five percent and sixty-two percent of Americans believe that aliens have landed on Earth. Surveys vary about the exact percentages, as does the look of the aliens. Some are green, some gray. Some have ears, some do not. All have large heads. The report reminded me of a survey I saw some years ago about the number of people who believe in the Devil. Not the devil as metaphor and not a generalized concept of evil; the Devil, one might say, as a creature of flesh and blood, someone who walks the earth, looks like us, and is inclined to offer sly temptations and unholy propositions. Believers have in mind, I think, something on the order of Stephen Vincent Benét's creation in *The Devil and Daniel Webster*. I can't remember the percentages the survey uncovered, but they were high. I can't remember because I have repressed the figure or, as the psychologists now say, gone into denial. Conventional wisdom tells us that going into denial is not healthful, even though it is obvious that doing so has many advantages. Ernest Becker explains some of them in his famous book *The Denial of Death*. But one does not have to go as deeply as Becker to make good use of denial. If you are an American writer who fancies himself an heir of the Enlightenment, it is hard to write three pages unless you

7

emphatically deny that many of your potential readers believe in deal-making devils.

Denial is also helpful when one begins to contemplate the mental condition of some important members of our intellectual elite. I refer to those who have fallen under the devilish spell of what is vaguely called "postmodernism," and in particular a subdivision of it sometimes called "deconstructionism." Academic responsibility requires me to give some detail about this worldview, and I will do so in a later chapter. Here, I need only remark that in this way of understanding things, language is under deep suspicion and is even thought to be delusional. Jean Baudrillard, a Frenchman, of all things, tells us that not only does language falsely represent reality, but there is no reality to represent. (Perhaps this explains, at long last, the indifferent French resistance to the German invasion of their country in World War II: They didn't believe it was real.) In an earlier time, the idea that language is incapable of mapping reality would have been considered nonsense, if not a form of mental illness. In fact, it *is* a form of mental illness. Nonetheless, in our own time the idea has become an organizing principle of prestigious academic departments. You can get a Ph.D. in this sort of thing.

There is, of course, a connection between alien- and devil-believers and a certain variety of deconstructionists. They are people in the thrall of a serious depression, and, in truth, it is unseemly to make fun of them, especially since most of us are suffering in varying degrees from the same malady. If I knew more about psychology, I might be able to give the sickness a name. Instead, I turn to poets—not for a name but for a confirmation and a cause. Yeats, for example, gives us a precise description of our wayward academics and our overcommitted alienites: The former lack all conviction, while the latter are full of passionate intensity. T. S. Eliot, you will remember, wrote of the hollow men occupying a wasteland. Auden wrote of the age of anxiety. Vachel Lindsay wrote of leaden-eyed people who have no gods to serve. Edna St. Vincent Millay, in her book *Huntsman, What Quarry?*, wrote a poem which goes to the root of the problem. Here is an excerpt:

> *Upon this gifted age, in its dark hour,*
> *Rains from the sky a meteoric shower*
> *Of facts . . . they lie unquestioned, uncombined.*
> *Wisdom enough to leech us of our ill*
> *Is daily spun; but there exists no loom*
> *To weave it into fabric.*

No loom to weave facts into fabric, people with no gods to serve, hollow and anxious, distrusting language, uncertain about even the most obvious features of reality, lacking conviction, suspicious of truth.

What are we to make of this? There are many possibilities. Among them are the strange and fanciful dreams that seem always to accompany the onset of a new millennium. Some believe a new age signals the Second Coming of Christ, some believe it signals the end of everything, and in between the varieties of delusion are legion. The possibility that strikes me as most plausible is more mundane. And it has happened before, with or without the coming of a new millennium. I refer to the confusion that accompanies the absence of a narrative to give organization and meaning to our world—a story of transcendence and mythic power. Nothing can be clearer than that we require a story to explain to ourselves why we are here and what our future is to be, and many other things, including where authority resides. I am not writing this book to document the loss of narrative. I have done that already, as have others in books bet-

9

ter than mine. Besides, I have no intention of writing still another depressing book about the breakdown of the human spirit. But it may be said here that when people do not have a satisfactory narrative to generate a sense of purpose and continuity, a kind of psychic disorientation takes hold, followed by a frantic search for something to believe in or, probably worse, a resigned conclusion that there is nothing to find. The devil-believers reclaim a fragment of the great narrative of Genesis. The alien-believers ask for deliverance from green-gray creatures whose physics has overcome the speed of light. The deconstructionists keep confusion at bay by writing books in which they tell us that there is nothing to write books about. There is even one group who seeks meaning in the ingenuity of technological innovation. I refer to those who, looking ahead, see a field of wonders encapsulated in the phrase "the information superhighway." They are information junkies, have no interest in narratives of the past, give little thought to the question of purpose. To the poet who asks, "Where is the loom to weave it all into fabric?," they reply that none is needed. To the poet who asks, "What gods do you serve?," they reply, "Those which make information accessible in great volume, at instantaneous speed, and in diverse forms." Such people have no hesitation in speaking of building a bridge to the new century. But to the question "What will we carry across the bridge?" they answer, "What else but high-definition TV, virtual reality, e-mail, the Internet, cellular phones, and all the rest that digital technology has produced?"

These, then, are the hollow men Eliot spoke of. They are, in a sense, no different from the alien- and devil-believers in that they have found a story that will keep them going for a while, but not for long. And, in a way, they are no different from those academics who find temporary amusement and professional advancement in having no story at all. I am not writing my book for these people. I write for those who are still searching for a way to confront the future, a way that faces reality as it is, that is connected to a humane tradition, that provides sane authority and meaningful purpose. I include myself among such people.

Where shall we look for such a way? Well, of course, one turns first to the wisdom of the sages, both near and far. Marcus Aurelius said, "At every action, no matter by whom preferred, make it a practice to ask yourself, 'What is his object in doing this?' But begin with yourself; put this question to yourself first of all." Goethe told us, "One should, each day, try to hear a little song, read a good poem, see a fine picture, and, if possible, speak a few reasonable words." Socrates said, "The unexamined life is not worth living." Rabbi Hillel said, "What is hateful to thee, do not do to another." The prophet Micah: "What does the Lord require of thee but to do justly, to love mercy and to walk humbly with Thy God." And our own Henry David Thoreau said, "All our inventions are but improved means to an unimproved end."

I could go on nearly endlessly with these quotations, since the wisdom of the ages and the sages is not bound by time and space. We may add to the list Confucius, Isaiah, Jesus, Muhammad, the Buddha, Shakespeare, Spinoza, and many more. What they tell us is all the same: There is no escaping from ourselves. The human dilemma is as it always has been, and it is a delusion to believe that the future will render irrelevant what we know and have long known about ourselves but find it convenient to forget.

How useful is it to be reminded? The words of the sages can calm and comfort us. They offer perspective and a release from the frenzy of speed and ambition. Very useful, I would say. But, of course, they are very far away from us in time and cultural conditions, and their advice is so abstract that it is difficult to see how we can turn much of it into practical and coherent instruction. In some parts of the Islamic world the commandments of Muhammad are, in fact, taken as imperatives of everyday life. And there are Christians and Jews who follow the Law down to the last detail. But for many of us, unsettled by the realities of vast change, especially technological change, fundamentalism of any kind rings hollow. We have problems and questions that Muhammad, Jesus, Hillel, Socrates, and Micah did not and could not speak of.

Let us take a small but clear example. Not long ago (as these things are measured) scientists in Scotland successfully cloned a sheep. Another group of scientists in America cloned a monkey and a cow. And apparently, an American high school student, in order to gain some extra credit, has claimed to have cloned a frog. We can expect, if not this year or the next, that the cloning of human beings will become a reality. I think we can say that we have here a genuine twenty-first-century problem. It would be interesting—wouldn't it?—to speculate on what Jesus or the Buddha would say about this development in human reproduction. But we will have to address the matter without them. How will we do that? Where will we go for guidance? What use shall we make of this technology? Who has an answer we will find acceptable?

Here is an answer I imagine all but a deconstructionist will find clearly unacceptable: Cloning humans opens up a whole new field of "human spare parts." The way it would work is that every time someone is born, a clone of this person would be made. The clone would be kept in a special, confined, and well-guarded place so that it can provide spare parts for the original person as needed throughout life. If the original person loses a kidney or lung at some time in his or her life, we would simply take it from the clone. Is there a problem with this? Well, of course, you will protest that the clone is, after all, a real human being. But that would only be the case if we *define* the clone as a human being.

There is nothing new in human beings' defining other human beings as non-human things. In all cases of genocide, that is exactly the procedure. Joseph Goebbels explained how to do such things. In our own times, Marvin Minsky and others working in the field of artificial intelligence have prophesied enthusiastically that humans will become merely pets of their computers, so that the definition of the worth and capacity of humans will change. We have never had clones before. Who is to say we cannot use them in the way I have suggested?

I hope you are thinking that my proposal is simply a bad joke and that any such proposal, seriously made, is a product of a depraved mind. I agree with you. But here is a question: Where did you get the idea that this proposal would be the product of a depraved mind? I imagine you believe that infanticide is also a depraved idea, in spite of the fact that it has been practiced for many more years in human history than it has been forbidden. Where did you get the idea that infanticide is horrible? Or that slavery is a bad idea? Or that the divine right of kings is a bad idea?

What I am driving at is that in order to have an agreeable encounter with the twenty-first century, we will have to take into it some good ideas. And in order to do that, we need to look back to take stock of the good ideas available to us. I am suspicious of people who want us to be forward-looking. I literally do not know what they mean when they say, "We must look ahead to see where we are going." What is it that they wish us to look at? There is nothing yet to see in the future. If looking ahead means anything, it must mean finding in our past useful and humane ideas with which to fill the future.

I do not mean—mind you—technological ideas, like going to the moon, airplanes, and antibiotics. We have no shortage of those ideas. I am referring to ideas of which we can say they have

13

advanced our understanding of ourselves, enlarged our definitions of humanness. Shall we look for some in the century that is
ending? What is there to find—the principle of indeterminacy?
Nietzsche's arguments for the death of God? Freud's insistence
that reason is merely a servant of the genitalia? The idea that language is utterly incapable of providing accurate maps of reality?
You may think that I am loading the case against the twentieth
century. Surely, you will call to mind (let us say, in America) the
rejection of the segregation of races, the rejection of the inferior-
ity of women, the increased access to higher education, and a few
other advances. But these were not truly twentieth-century ideas,
but rather extensions of ideas that arose at an earlier time. If you
put your mind to it, I suppose you can recall several ideas that
originated in our own century, and that will be useful in the next.
But if you think too long, you are on a road to despair. Is it not
obvious that our century has been an almost unrelieved horror?
Who would have thought, in 1900—the year, by the way, of
Nietzsche's death and the publication of Freud's *The Interpretation of Dreams*—that the twentieth century would feature continuous mass murder, far exceeding anything humanity had
witnessed in the previous two millennia? Who would have
thought that the three great transcendent narratives of this century would be fascism, nazism, and communism? Who would
have thought weapons would be invented that, in a flash, could
end all human life? Who would have thought that the theme of
this century would be "Technology Über Alles"? I am sorry to say
it, but I don't think we will get much help from our own century.
As you can tell, I speak as an enemy of this century. But even if
you are not, you must admit it is hard to be its friend.

If we are looking for good ideas that may be revived,
enhanced, appropriately modified, we could do worse than cast

our eye on the fifth century B.C.—the time of the great Athenians. I know that they are the classic example of Dead White Males, but we probably should pay them some attention anyway. These are the people who invented the idea of political democracy. They invented what we call Western philosophy and what we call logic and rhetoric. They came very close to inventing what we call science, and one of them—Epicurus, by name—conceived of the atomic theory of matter 2,300 years before it occurred to any modern scientist. They wrote and performed plays that, almost three millennia later, still have the power to make audiences laugh and weep. They even invented what today we call the Olympics, and among their values none stood higher than that in all things one should strive for excellence.

But for all of this, their most luminous intellect, Plato, was the world's first systematic fascist. The Greeks saw nothing wrong in having slaves or in killing infants (although Aristotle opposed the latter). Their conception of democracy relegated women to silence and anonymity. And they despised foreigners. Their word for those who could not speak Greek was "barbarian." They were also technological innocents, a serious limitation if technological people wish to learn from them. The Athenians produced no important technical inventions, and they could not even devise ways of using horsepower efficiently.

In sum, while it is not possible to ignore completely the contribution Athens made to our journey toward humanity, the Athenians are too far from us and too strange and too insular and too unacquainted with the power of technology for us to use their ideas as a social or intellectual paradigm. In the third century, Tertullian, one of the Church Fathers, asked a famous question: "What has Athens to do with Jerusalem?" It was rhetorical; he meant Athens had nothing to do with Jerusalem. In the twenty-first century, we may vary the question and modify the answer: What has Athens to do with New York (or London or Paris)? The answer: Much less than we would wish. The same may be said for the Middle Ages—in my opinion a much-maligned era. We ought to remember that Robert Maynard Hutchins used the medieval period and its ideas as a guide for education when he reformed the University of Chicago in the nineteen-thirties and -forties. He did so because he found a very high degree of integration in the world-view of the Middle Ages. Medieval theologians developed an elaborate and systematic description of our relationship to God, to nature, to each other, and to our tools. Their theology took as a first and last principle that all knowledge and goodness come from God and that, therefore, all human enterprise must be directed toward the service of God. Theology, not technology, provided people with authorization for what to do and think. That is why Leonardo kept his design of a submarine secret, believing, as he did, that it would not gain favor in God's eyes. It is why Pope Innocent II prohibited the use of the crossbow, claiming it was "hateful to God" and could not be used against Christians. Of course, he saw no problem in using it against infidels. But the point is that in the theocratic world-view, technology was not autonomous but was subject to the jurisdiction of a binding religious system. Can you imagine anyone saying today that cloning humans should be prohibited because it would not find favor in God's eyes? Well, of course, some people do say that, but we are inclined to discredit them as naive fundamentalists or fanatics. Which is why I think the medieval way can offer us only minimal guidance. In a theocratic world, everyone is a fundamentalist. In a technological world, and in a multicultural world, fundamentalism is a side issue, confined to those places that are still theocratic and are therefore regarded as a danger to world harmony.

This question—Where shall we look for guidance about what to do and think in the twenty-first century, especially guidance about our relationship to technology?—is as significant as it is daunting, especially hard for those who are strangers to history. "Every culture," Lewis Mumford once wrote, "lives within its dream." But we often lose our dream, as I believe happened to us in the twentieth century. And we are in danger if we cannot reclaim one that will help us go forward. What else is history for if not to remind us about our better dreams?

With this in mind, I suggest that we turn our attention to the eighteenth century. It is *there*, I think, that we may find ideas that offer a humane direction to the future, ideas that we can carry with confidence and dignity across the bridge to the twenty-first century. They are not strange ideas. They are still close to us. They are not all that difficult to remember. I suggest we try to reclaim some of them, with this provision: I am not suggesting that we *become* the eighteenth century, only that we use it for what it is worth and for all it is worth. In the preface to one of the many editions of *Democracy in America,* Tocqueville urged his fellow countrymen and -women to pay attention to America the way I would urge we pay attention to the eighteenth century. If I may adapt his thought and almost all of his words, I would put it this way: Let us not turn to the eighteenth century in order to copy the institutions she fashioned for herself but in order that we may better understand what suits us. Let us look there for instruction rather than models. Let us adopt the principles rather than the details.

Who and what will we find there? The eighteenth century is the century of Goethe, Voltaire, Rousseau, Diderot, Kant, Hume, Gibbon, Pestalozzi, and Adam Smith. It is the century of Thomas Paine, Jefferson, Adams, and Franklin. In the eighteenth century we developed our ideas about inductive science,

17

about religious and political freedom, about popular education, about rational commerce, and about the nation-state. In the eighteenth century, we also invented the idea of progress, and, you may be surprised to know, our modern idea of happiness. It was in the eighteenth century that reason began its triumph over superstition. And, inspired by Newton, who was elected president of the Royal Society at the beginning of the century, writers, musicians, and artists conceived of the universe as orderly, rational, and comprehensible. Beethoven composed his First Symphony in the eighteenth century, and we should not be surprised that Bach, Handel, Mozart, and Haydn composed their music in the eighteenth century. Or that Schiller, Swift, Defoe, Fielding, Samuel Johnson, Voltaire, and William Blake were among its major writers. Or that Gainsborough, Hogarth, David, and Reynolds were its best-known painters.

We are talking about the time referred to as our period of Enlightenment. In truth, it may be said to begin toward the middle of the seventeenth century with the ideas of John Locke and Newton, and extend into the nineteenth if we wish to include— as I think we ought to—the ideas of John Stuart Mill and Alexis de Tocqueville and the great Romantic poets. And so the eighteenth century is a kind of metaphor referring to the time, as Kant put it, when we achieved our release from our self-imposed tutelage. It is the time of which historians have said that the battle for free thought was begun and won. By the end of that time, the modern world had been created. This is the century which Isaiah Berlin summed up in these words: "The intellectual power, honesty, lucidity, courage and disinterested love of the truth of the most gifted thinkers of the eighteenth century remain to this day without parallel. Their age is one of the best and most hopeful episodes in the life of mankind."[1]

If this is so, we can hardly afford to neglect it, which is why I recommend it to your notice, your study, and your advocacy. In chapters that follow, I will try to show how some of the ideas of the eighteenth century may be useful to us. But I must say, here, especially because the thought has probably occurred to you, that I am well aware that there existed inhumane beliefs and institutions in that century. The burning of witches was still taking place. France burned its last witch in 1746, Germany in 1775, and Poland in 1793. In Italy, the tortures of the Inquisition continued until the end of the century. Slavery still existed, at least in America. The oppression of women was standard practice, as was child labor. And, of course, most nations were still ruled by despots. But it was in the eighteenth century that the arguments were generated that made these inhumanities both visible and, in the end, insupportable. Yes, Jefferson had slaves. But he knew that he *shouldn't* have slaves. He proposed, unsuccessfully, a denunciation of the African slave trade in the Declaration of Independence, urged that it be prohibited in Virginia, and was well aware that one of his predecessors as President had freed his slaves, and that the other would have found it unthinkable to have slaves. Yes, Frederick the Great ruled Prussia with an iron hand. But he employed the greatest enemy of despotism, Voltaire, as his court philosopher. If you can imagine it, this would be analogous to Lenin's employing John D. Rockefeller to teach him economic theory. Yes, women were considered second-class citizens, but it was in the eighteenth century that Mary Wollstonecraft wrote a *Vindication of the Rights of Women*, perhaps, even today, the best-known feminist tract. Yes, children as young as seven or eight worked from sunup to sundown in factories and mines. But the idea that child labor is inhumane came from the eighteenth century, in particular from Rousseau, who

19

gave us the idea that children must have a childhood. And yes, Thomas Paine's *The Age of Reason*, which was an uncompromising attack on the Bible and churches of all kinds, led to his being vilified and denied his rightful place among America's Founding Fathers. But the First Amendment to the American Constitution nonetheless forbade any interference with people's religious beliefs.

You can take any century you please and make a list of its inhumanities. The eighteenth is no exception. But it is *there*, and in no other, that we have the beginnings of much that is worthwhile about the modern world.

Chapter Two

Progress

In the middle of the eighteenth century (1750 to be exact) Jean-Jacques Rousseau threw away his watch. "Thank Heavens," he said, "I shall no longer need to know what time it is."[1] But he knew what time it was. It was a time of spectacular advances in science and technology. In the eighteenth century, Fahrenheit invented the mercury thermometer, inoculations against smallpox began, Stephen Hales figured out how to measure blood pressure, Lavoisier discovered that air consists mostly of oxygen and nitrogen, Linnaeus created his great scientific taxonomies. And, of course, as we all used to learn in school, James Watt perfected the steam engine.

All of this knowledge and its technological manifestations were the outgrowth of what we now call "rationalism." Rousseau is the figure we most quickly associate with a reaction *against* rationalism, and, as his discarding his watch suggests, he was particularly hostile to precision in measurement, which was a hallmark of the rational and scientific world-view. When we speak of "Romanticism," we speak of a rejection of the presumptions of rationalism, an important idea for people like ourselves to consider—but only after we are clear about what rationalism is, or at least was, in the eighteenth century. There are those among us today who fancy themselves to be within the rationalist tradition but who are in fact strangers to it. It is worthwhile to review the matter with some care.

To begin, rationalism was a denial of the Christian belief in the supernatural and, therefore, a rejection of God. This is not to say that all or even most of the eighteenth-century rationalists turned irrevocably away from Christianity or God. Revolutions in thought are never simple, and in any case God is not so easy to dispose of. We might say that most rationalists turned against theology and priests rather than spirituality and God. Which means that there were continuous intellectual and emotional negotiations between rationalists and Christianity, many of the former calling themselves Deists. For example, Voltaire, in denouncing what he called "the Ecclesiastical Ministry," wrote: "The institution of religion exists only to keep mankind in order, and to make men merit the goodness of God by their virtue. Everything in a religion which does not tend toward this goal must be considered alien or dangerous."[2] This does not sound like a man who hates God, only organized religion. And the same might be said for Thomas Jefferson. He was accused repeatedly of being an atheist, in part because he wrote a version of the Gospels in which he removed all of the supernatural elements, retaining only the ethical principles (as did, by the way, Hegel in his *Life of Jesus*). In Jefferson's account, Jesus emerges as the best man who ever lived, but lacking the status of divinity. At no time did Jefferson declare a disbelief in God.[3] Perhaps the clearest example of a Deistic rationalist is Thomas Paine, whose book *The Age of Reason* is the best-known attack on the authority and purpose of religious systems. For all that, it contains this sentence: "I believe in one God, and no more; and I hope for happiness beyond this life."[4]

The relationship between rationalism and Christianity is a very complex one, expressed with some irony in Crane Brinton's remark that "the Enlightenment is a child of Christianity—which may explain for our Freudian times why the Enlightenment was so hostile to Christianity."[5] I will refer, in a while, to the connection between rationalism and Christianity in the context of the idea of progress. Here, it is sufficient to say that rationalism was essentially a revolt against orthodoxy, and since the Christian world-view was the principal orthodoxy of the time, it was inevitable that it would be the target of continuous attack. But it was very far from the only target. Superstition in its various forms, especially what we may call inherited superstition, was ridiculed, followed closely by the idea of monarchy. Rationalistic attacks on monarchy were unrelenting and effective, resulting in the gradual erosion of the divine right of kings and the unlimited authority of monarchs. Denis Diderot combined attacks on both monarchy and religion in his famous remark, "Men will never be free till the last king is strangled with the entrails of the last priest."[6] One may get a less heated idea of the arguments against monarchy by reading John Locke, although the most dramatic presentation of the case against it is, of course, the American Declaration of Independence. I particularly like the way Ulrich Im Hof put the result. "Any monarch," he wrote, "however despotic, found it worthwhile to masquerade as an enlightened ruler, to behave more like a schoolteacher than a tyrant."[7] But by the end of the eighteenth century, even the schoolteacher role was deemed unjustifiable and, as we know, the Enlightenment produced two great republics—the United States and France. And more would follow.

However we may define rationalism, it is clear we are talking about a radical reorientation in the way people thought about the world. Superstition, inherited "wisdom," obedience to tradition, and supernatural metaphysics fell before the assumed power and authority of reason. Ernst Cassirer remarks that the eighteenth century is "imbued with the belief in the unity and immutability of reason. Reason is the same for all thinking subjects, all nations, all epochs, and all cultures."[8] And Brinton defines rationalism as a "cluster of ideas adding up to the belief that the universe works the way a man's mind works when he is thinking logically and objectively."[9]

It follows from this that the freedom, confidence, and radicalism of rationalist thought created fertile conditions for the growth of natural science. The following quotation from Voltaire is typical in its expression of just such a sense of freedom, confidence, and radicalism. Of course, since no one (with the possible exception of Paine) wrote with a brilliance and lucidity to match Voltaire's, it is also atypical:

> Wretched human beings, whether you wear green robes, black robes or surplices, cloaks and clerical bands, never seek to use authority where it is only a question of reason, unless you wish to be scoffed at throughout the centuries as the most impertinent of men, and to suffer public hatred as the most unjust.
>
> You have been spoken to a hundred times of the insolent absurdity with which you condemned Galileo, and I speak to you for the hundred and first, and I hope you will keep the anniversary of that event forever. Would that there might be graved on the door of your Holy Office: "Here seven cardinals, assisted by minor brethren, had the finest thinker of Italy thrown into prison at the age of seventy; made him fast on bread and water because he instructed the human race, and because they were ignorant."[10]

It is not true, as some rationalists believed, that science originated in the eighteenth century and that the Middle Ages provide no examples of rational science. Condillac, an atheistic abbé of the eighteenth century, dismissed the Middle Ages as "centuries of ignorance." Condorcet acknowledged that medieval scientists gave us the compass and gunpowder but believed they made themselves ridiculous by their obsession with astrology and alchemy. And even Rousseau found the "scientific jargon" of the Middle Ages "more contemptible than ignorance." In fact, medieval scientists—Roger Bacon, for example—did useful work in technology, optics, and medicine; and Galileo's research relied to some extent on methodological principles developed in the thirteenth and fourteenth centuries. It is also true that the seventeenth century was a time of scientific genius. In fact, we may say that it saw the beginning of modern science. Kepler, Galileo, and Tycho Brahe may have been "sleepwalkers" (i.e., had no idea where their studies were leading), as Arthur Koestler called them, but, asleep or not, they walked in the direction of what we now think of as inductive science. Thus, the best way to put it is to say that by 1700 the natural sciences had reached a stage which made Newton's synthesis possible. That stage reached, the great possibilities of science came into view, a vision made sharper by the accomplishments of the Encyclopedists, who attempted to gather together in an organized, systematic way all the reliable knowledge of their day. Diderot, the originator of the *Encyclopédie*, described its purpose as both supplying knowledge and effecting a change in the way people thought. Reliable knowledge was to be the arsenal of reason, and reason would be the force which led to rational change.

In this state of mind, it was inevitable that the rationalists would develop a theory of progress. In using the phrase "a theory of progress" I am aware of its strangeness. To most of us, progress is not a theory; it is a fact. Perhaps not a fact of nature (although Darwin's theory suggests that it is), but a fact of human history. As Dr. Johnson thought that by kicking a stone he refuted Bishop Berkeley's claim that matter does not exist, we think we may refute any doubts about the fact of progress by picking up a telephone, taking an aspirin, or flying to London. But people have not always thought that progress was a fact, natural or otherwise. Scholars have searched as far back as biblical times and the fifth century B.C. to find evidence of a general notion of the continuous improvement of human life on earth, and have been hard put to find any. Mind you, we are not talking here about a concept of "better." All peoples have notions of improvement, of superior/inferior. What is at issue here is the following (I quote from J. B. Bury's famous book *The Idea of Progress*): ". . . an interpretation of history which regards men as slowly advancing . . . in a definite and desirable direction, and infers that this progress will continue indefinitely."[11]

It is generally believed that in the classical period of Greece and Rome there did not exist a clear idea of progress as an inevitable and immutable movement of history. We find, rather, what may be called cyclical theories—a golden age declining to a silver age, a silver age to an iron age, which is eventually succeeded by a new golden age. The idea of decadence is as strong and ever-present as the idea of progress. And this view of humankind's journey is even a feature of the Renaissance in its excessive admiration for classical antiquity, especially ancient Rome. It has been argued that a concept of progress can be found in the Hebrew Bible—in the words of Isaiah, for example—and in the Christian world-view as expressed in several places, especially by John in Revelation. But in neither of these traditions is there a notion of progress comparable to that which was developed during the Enlightenment. In the Christian cosmology, man was at his best in a state of innocence; that is, before the Fall.

Eden can never be reclaimed on Earth, and only through a transcendent miracle, not by historical processes, can salvation be achieved. Heaven, and nowhere else, is where perfection will be found. But to many of the Rationalists, Heaven can wait. Happiness and peace and moral rectitude will be established here on Earth. And this can be done through the power of reason, which will do for all people what it allowed Newton and Locke to do: to understand the universe, to shape the environment, to control nature and themselves.

Of course, the origin of such a view predates the eighteenth century by quite a bit and is sometimes attributed to Descartes, sometimes to Machiavelli, but more often to Francis Bacon (to whom Bury gives great attention and credit in *The Idea of Progress*). Bacon was born in 1561 and died in 1626, and if we may say that Newton and Locke were the fathers of the Enlightenment, Bacon might be called its grandfather. Although Bacon had no coherent theory concerning the movement of civilization, he is the first to claim that the principal end of scientific work was to advance the "happiness of mankind." He continually criticized his predecessors for failing to understand that the real, legitimate, and only goal of the sciences is the "endowment of human life with new inventions and riches." Many scientists who followed Bacon—for example, Kepler (who was born ten years after Bacon), Galileo, and even Newton—did not view science in the same way. The science they created was almost wholly concerned with questions of truth, not power. These men were not concerned with the idea of progress, and did not believe that their speculations held the promise of any important improvement in the conditions of life. It is Bacon who brought science down from the heavens, including mathematics, which he conceived of as a humble handmaiden to invention. Bacon, in short, was the chief architect of a new edifice of thought in which resignation and decadence were cast out. The name of his building was Progress and Power.

By the eighteenth century, the idea that history itself was moving inexorably toward a more peaceful, intelligent, and commodious life for mankind was widely held. Both David Hume and Adam Smith argued that there existed a self-generating impulse of rising expectations that must lead to a society of continuous improvement. Bernard Mandeville argued that the "private vices" of envy and pride are, in fact, "public virtues" in that they stimulate industry and invention, and Hume wrote that the "pleasures of luxury and the profit of commerce roused men from their indolence," leading them to advances in their various enterprises. If any of this sounds something like what has been called, in our own time, "Reaganism," it is because it was chiefly the eighteenth century that provided Reagan with his ideas, especially those arguments which give to ambition and even greed a moral dimension. The most extreme case for the virtues inherent in self-interest economics was made by Thomas Robert Malthus in his *Essay on the Principle of Population*, published in 1798. Malthus argued against ameliorating the lot of the poor, on the grounds that an easier life led the poor to have more children, which led to fewer material resources to go around, which led to everybody being worse off. Of course, by this logic the best policy was to allow the poor among us to starve—a position which, happily, has not been pursued rigorously in the West.

But the point here is not that reason is unerring (although when it errs, reason itself, it is alleged, can detect its own errors). The point is that in every field—economics, politics, religion, law, and, of course, science—reason was to be employed as the best means of assisting history's inevitable movement toward progress. Montesquieu, in *The Spirit of the Laws*, attempted to describe the process by which law improves. Adam Smith, in *The Wealth of Nations*, showed how we advance economically. Thomas Paine showed how the rights of man will and must expand. Vico, Pope, Bentham, Jefferson, and others were engaged in similar efforts toward revealing the felicitous movement of history. (For all of the current discussion about Jefferson's ambiguous attitudes about slavery, he had no doubt that the future would be free of it.) And, of course, no one doubted that the future of science would reveal greater and still greater truths about nature. Here, for example, is an excerpt from a letter by Benjamin Franklin to Joseph Priestley (who, with Karl Wilhelm Steele, discovered oxygen, although Lavoisier coined the word). The letter was sent in February 1780, and conveys the sense of optimism about the future that was characteristic of the age:

> . . . I always rejoice to hear of your being still employed in experimental researches into nature, and the success you meet with. The rapid progress true science now makes, occasions my regretting sometimes that I was born too soon. It is impossible to imagine the height to which may be carried, in a thousand years, the power of man over matter.[12]

But for all of this optimism and for all of the successes brought by the application of reason, somewhere about the middle of the century a radically different note was sounded. And its first dissonant blast came from Rousseau, who did more than simply throw away his watch. What he did in a series of novels, philosophical tracts, and essays, as well as a famous autobiography, was to express a revulsion against all that reason brings, including the idea of progress. Before outlining his position I must interject that those with whom Rousseau quarreled were far

29

from fanatical about the uses of reason and the inevitability of progress. For example, there were those who while following the logic of Malthus's argument were repulsed by its heartlessness. And there were those who rejected the extremes—in some cases, totalitarianism or utopianism—to which reason seemed to lead. We are indebted to Montesquieu, Voltaire, Diderot, Condorcet, and, of course, Jefferson, Madison, and Washington, for their calm and balanced sense of reason which led us, in the long run, to modern liberal societies. Nonetheless, Rousseau became their enemy, both philosophically and personally. Diderot judged him to be deceitful, cruel, and hypocritical. Hume, who once admired him, later thought him an egotistical monster. To Frederick Melchior Grimm, Rousseau was odious, and to Voltaire, a monster of vanity and vileness. On the other hand, Kant believed Rousseau's sensibility of soul to be perfect, Percy Shelley called him a sublime genius, and Schiller thought him Christlike.[13] These opinions reflect the two sides of a great dispute that arose in the eighteenth century, a dispute, I might add, which has some relevance to our own situation.

The dispute is usually referred to as "Romanticism versus Rationalism." As with all such dichotomies, this is an oversimplification, and whomever you would put on one side might make claims for being more properly on the other. Rousseau himself, the standard-bearer of the Romantic movement, provides in *The Social Contract* a careful analysis of the roots of authority and social obedience, which is to say his arguments take a rationalistic form. Moreover, he wrote an entry on "political economy" for the *Encyclopédie;* and his *Emile,* a tract on education, takes the view of a standard-brand rationalist attacking the Church for its encouragement of superstition and its cult of miracles.

Rousseau, in other words, was a child of Rationalism—and yet, clearly, its most disobedient and disruptive child. He began his assault in 1749 by seeking a prize offered by the Academy of Dijon for an essay on the question "Has the Progress of the Sciences and the Arts contributed to corrupt, or to purify, morality?" His essay won the prize and, even better, made him famous. In it, he argued that culture itself is more evil than good. He ridiculed the alleged "advances" of civilization. He spoke of the confusion printing had produced. He spoke of how philosophy contributes to moral decay. He argued that reflection itself is unnatural, and that a thinking man is a depraved animal. He continued his objections to the spirit of the age in his novel *Héloise*, in *Emile*, and in his autobiography, *Confessions* (which, in fact, was published after his death). Rousseau placed himself on the side of religion and spirituality and of the significance of the life of feeling. Reason, he thought, argues against God and immortality, but feeling is in favor of both. Materialism and atheism, he claimed, went hand in hand, and he thought them demeaning to the human spirit.

By the time he was through, Rousseau had created what might be called the cult of nature; had revealed the limitations of reason, and effectively championed the superiority of poetic insight and intuition; had raised his culture's consciousness of the uniqueness of childhood; had amplified the importance of the individual, far beyond where the Renaissance had taken it; and, we might say, had fathered modern introspective literature.

Rousseau's heirs, of whom Shelley was among the most famous, matured in the nineteenth century and, in doing so, provided the world with some of its most sublime, profound, and beautiful poetry. Wordsworth, Keats, Blake, Coleridge, Byron, Schiller, Goethe, Heine, Hugo, Baudelaire, and, of course, Shelley himself are among those we think of as great Romantic poets. But Shelley did more than write poetry. He also wrote *about* poetry, specifically a 10,000-word essay which was to intellectual life what the Declaration of Independence was to political life. He called the essay "In Defense of Poetry," and in it he made the arguments that explained why Reason itself was insufficient to produce humane progress. Scientific and technological advances could proceed without an ethical basis. But that is not the case with social progress. Indeed, when science and technology claim to provide ethical imperatives, we are led into moral catastrophe. Shelley used as illustrations of his point the Terror that accompanied the French Revolution, and the Napoleonic dictatorship. He wrote his essay in 1821. Had he been writing it in 1944, the Holocaust would have served even better. It is only through love, tenderness, and beauty, he wrote, that the mind is made receptive to moral decency, and poetry is the means by which love, tenderness, and beauty are best cultivated. It is the poetic imagination, not scientific accomplishment, that is the engine of moral progress. "The great instrument of moral good," he wrote, "is the imagination; and poetry administers to the effect by acting on the cause." Thus, the "heavenly city" that the eighteenth-century rationalists dreamed of is not reachable through reason alone, and history will turn an angry face toward a society that relies on it. Progress is the business of the heart, not the intellect.

And so the great argument about the source of social progress became a significant feature of the Enlightenment. But it is necessary to say at once that a belief in moral and political progress as either inevitable or (at least) possible was retained well into the nineteenth century, and for very good reasons. It is true (on the other hand) that the Reign of Terror, almost by itself, cast a pall over hopes for the future. The eighteenth century, which Carlyle hated passionately, gave us the guillotine, the first mechanized form of execution; it removed, more or less neatly, 20,000 heads. It is also true that the mechanization of industry led to both the disruption and the corruption of community life, and, in England, gave us laws that rewarded with the death penalty those who would destroy machinery. It is even true that the Enlightenment's greatest intellects—Voltaire and Kant—were (as we would say today) anti-Semites. Kant thought the Jews "a nation of cheats," and Voltaire, in his *Philosophical Dictionary*, speaks of Jews as contemptible, largely, one might add, because they are the people who created the conditions for Christianity. Thus, it would seem possible that even the most avid advocates of the dignity of the individual can harbor primitive beliefs. To which we might add Jefferson, who in his *Notes on Virginia* explains why "Negroes" are inferior to whites and apparently always will be.

Granting, then, that there were reasons for a less-than-optimistic view of the future, especially as we would see such deficiencies today, the case for a belief in the march of progress was nonetheless strong. From 1815 to 1853, there were no major wars in Europe. The American experiment in political democracy was holding fast. Serfs were freed in Russia, slavery was abolished in English colonies and would soon be in America. The status of women was being redefined, belief in witchcraft was diminishing, horrific methods of punishment were disappearing. Religious freedom in England and America was a fact. The assumptions of our modern views of children and their education began to take form. Johann Pestalozzi, a Swiss educator, took Rousseau's ideas about children seriously and put them into practice. His student, Friedrich Froebel, who is the originator of early childhood education, invented the kindergarten, opening his first school in 1837. Based to a considerable extent on Rousseau's image of childhood, laws were enacted to protect children, the necessity for which is hard for people like ourselves to conceive. Consider: In 1761, an Englishwoman named Ann Martin was convicted of putting out the eyes of children with whom she went begging about the country. She was sentenced to a mere two years in Newgate Prison, and most likely would not have been convicted at all if the children had been her own. Her crime, it would appear, consisted in damaging the property of others. But by 1814, legislation had been introduced that would have sent Martin to jail for a much longer time, and, in fact, the law made stealing a child an indictable offense for the first time in English history. It should also be mentioned that the significance of the discovery of bacteria by Antoni van Leeuwenhoek in 1676 began to be grasped in the eighteenth century, resulting in improvements in sewage and the disposal of waste. And, to go from the mundane to the sublime, Immanuel Kant's influential work *The Critique of Practical Reason* argued for the view that morality is present in the intuition of our practical reason. We do not have to discover a new morality; we need only to recover that which is already at hand, thus suggesting that our moral universe is more familiar, accessible, and practical than is usually believed.

It would be possible to write a whole book—in fact, several—on how and why faith in progress could be maintained, although for different reasons, by both rationalists and romantics, especially as the West moved deep into the nineteenth century. Rationalists would find evidence in the obvious advances in science and technology, increased political and religious freedom, the decline of monarchies, the rise of republics, and the "proof" that Darwinian evolution gave to the doctrine of progress. Romantics, for all of their skepticism, could take heart from examples of moral progress, such as the decline of slavery, the elevation of women, the growth of the concept of childhood, and a new appreciation of nature.

The idea of progress, then, is one of the great gifts of the Enlightenment. The eighteenth century invented it, elaborated it, and promoted it, and in so doing generated vast resources of vitality, confidence, and hope. But the eighteenth century also criticized and doubted it, initiating powerful arguments about its limitations and pitfalls. This fact is often neglected by those among us who claim that we have come to the end of the Enlightenment. Or who claim that the eighteenth-century faith in reason has led us into twentieth-century disaster. To take the most dreadful example of the claim: In his book *Modernity and the Holocaust*, Zygmunt Bauman argues that the Holocaust was an extension of faith in reason. "The 'Final Solution,'" he writes, "did not clash at any stage with the rational pursuit of efficient, optimal goal-implementation. On the contrary, *it arose out of a genuinely rational concern and it was generated by bureaucracy true to its form and purpose*" (italics his).[14] But this argument is not much different from Rousseau's. Reason, when unaided and untempered by poetic insight and humane feeling, turns ugly and dangerous. Blake, Carlyle, Ruskin, and William Morris agreed. And their saying so is part of the gift of the Enlightenment.

We must remember this if we seek assistance from those who gave us the modern world.

Chapter Three

Technology

No, it is not quite right to say that progress was a gift of the eighteenth century. It is more accurate and (as it happens) more useful to say that the eighteenth century, having invented the idea, then proceeded to express doubts about it in the form of significant questions: What is progress? How does it happen? How is it corrupted? What is the relationship between technological and moral progress?

The gift of the eighteenth century is to be found in the intelligence and vigor of the questions it raised about progress, a fact that was well understood by the best minds of the century that followed. In the nineteenth century, these questions were addressed, and full and passionate answers came forth, especially about the connection between technological and moral progress. William Blake wrote of the "dark satanic mills" which stripped men of their souls. He insisted that passivity in the face of the alleged movement of "progress" leads to psychic slavery. Matthew Arnold warned that "faith in machinery" was humankind's greatest menace. Ruskin, William Morris, and Carlyle railed against the spiritual degradation brought by industrial progress. Balzac, Flaubert, and Zola documented in their novels the spiritual emptiness that a culture obsessed with progress produces.

Technology

We can get a clear idea of the seriousness and skepticism with which European intellectuals regarded technological progress by reading a letter Lord Byron sent prior to a speech he gave to the House of Lords early in the nineteenth century. The letter summarizes his speech. He spoke against a proposed law which would apply the death penalty to anyone deliberately breaking a machine, as those people called "Luddites" were in the habit of doing. Byron tried to show how the rise of factories made workers useless and desperate, and how their way of life was being destroyed. Byron was not a Luddite himself, and, in fact, understood the advantages of mechanized progress. But he saw in such progress a tainted bargain—economic growth on one hand, the loss of self-respect and community vitality on the other. (The law was passed, with only three votes against it.)

Excerpts from Byron's letter, sent to Lord Holland in 1812, will be found in Appendix I to this book. I recommend it to you, and suggest further that you compare it to the way in which Al Gore speaks of the future of computer technology. Or Alvin Toffler. Or George Gilder. Or Nicholas Negroponte. Or, for that matter, the average school superintendent who believes that computers will, at long last, solve the problem of how to educate children. Rousseau would have laughed at that, as would have Pestalozzi, the greatest educator of the eighteenth century. Voltaire would have written of it with his customary bile.

Of course, there were those, especially in America, who thought that technological progress would foster moral progress, among them Emerson, whose enthusiasm for the future led to his famous remark that "the golden age is before, not behind us." Mark Twain, fascinated by the technical accomplishments of the nineteenth century, judged his century to be "the plainest and sturdiest and infinitely greatest and worthiest of all the centuries the world has seen." And he once congratulated Walt Whitman on having lived in the age that gave the world the beneficial products of coal tar. Alexis de Tocqueville, skeptical of many things he saw in America, believed that technology might bring an end to "the disease of work," and he was somewhat in awe of the "lust for the new" that characterized the American spirit. There were more than a few who envisioned a golden age in the form of "utopian" communities—Robert Owen, for example, who, having founded an experimental community in Scotland, came to America to found another utopia, in 1825, at New Harmony, Indiana. Although none of his or other such experiments endured, dozens were tried in an effort to blend technological advances with moral uplift.

There is no question that to many nineteenth-century Americans, technology was clearly the engine of spiritual progress. Thoreau, the American Rousseau, didn't agree, but his objections went largely unnoticed, as did Thoreau himself. Also unnoticed was the message of many of Mark Twain's novels, especially *A Connecticut Yankee in King Arthur's Court* and his masterpiece, *Adventures of Huckleberry Finn.* For all of Twain's enthusiasm for the giantism of American industry, the totality of his work is an affirmation of pre-technological values. Personal loyalty, regional tradition, the continuity of family life, the relevance of the tales and wisdom of the elderly, are the soul of his books throughout. The story of Huck and Jim making their way to freedom on a raft is nothing less than a celebration of the enduring spirituality of pre-technological man. But not much of this perspective made a difference to Americans. Technological innovation filled the air with the promise of new freedoms and new forms of social organization.

And, of course, something of that spirit was to be found, across the sea, in the revolutionary thought of Karl Marx, a true child of the Enlightenment and a believer in history's movement toward progress. Although it seems ironic to say it, Marx's faith in progress received support from nineteenth-century biologists and geologists who promoted and "proved" the notion of organic evolution. History may or may not be moving toward the triumph of the proletariat, but it became clear from the research of geologists that life had progressed from bacteria to humans, from simplicity to complexity, from instinct to consciousness. Although Darwin's theory of evolution (whose leading principle was, in Huxley's phrase, "the survival of the fittest") was by no means entirely optimistic, it seemed clear to many in the nineteenth century that progress was as real as gravity or any other natural phenomenon. And its reality was given special force by the great invention of the nineteenth century: the invention of invention. We learned *how* to invent things, and the question of *why* receded in importance. The idea that if something could be done, it should be done was born in the nineteenth century. And along with it there developed a profound belief in all the principles through which invention succeeds: objectivity, efficiency, expertise, standardization, measurement, a market economy, and, of course, faith in progress. As a consequence, the nineteenth century produced a massive array of startling and culture-wracking inventions: telegraphy, photography, the rotary press, the telephone, the typewriter, the phonograph, the transatlantic cable, the electric light, movies, the locomotive, rockets, the steamboat, the x-ray, the revolver, and the stethoscope, not to mention canned food, the penny press, the modern magazine, the advertising agency, the modern bureaucracy, and even (although some dispute it) the safety pin.

I could fill the next two pages with other nineteenth-century inventions, including, by the way, the computer. In 1822, Charles Babbage announced that he had invented a machine capable of performing simple arithmetical calculations, and, in 1833, he produced a programmable machine that is the forerunner of the modern computer.

All of these inventions were a legacy of the Enlightenment and its idea that progress is assisted—indeed, given expression—by the application of reason. But the nineteenth century also carried forward eighteenth-century skepticism about progress, particularly the doubt that technological progress goes hand in hand with moral progress. I do not intend here a review of the nineteenth century, but it is necessary to say that, for all of its technological advances, the nineteenth century still had identifiable traces of the spiritual texture of the Enlightenment. The fury of industrialism was too new and as yet too limited in scope to alter the needs of inner life or to drive from memory the questions raised in the eighteenth century. In studying nineteenth-century America, for example, one can almost hear the groans of religion in crisis, of mythologies under attack, of a politics and education in confusion. But the groans are not yet death throes.

But something happened, as we know, in the twentieth century. Among other things, the idea that progress is real, humane, and inevitable died. As early as 1932, Lewis Mumford thought progress to be "the deadest of dead ideas . . . the one notion that has been thoroughly blasted by the twentieth-century experience."[1] Even before Mumford, Dean William Ralph Inge, in 1920, announced that the idea had lost its hold on our minds. It is hard to know why these men took this view so early in the century. Did Nietzsche and Freud give them a clue? Was it the senseless slaughter of World War I? Did they foresee the tyranny of communism and fascism? There is no point, I think, in documenting, at this late hour, what Mumford called our twentieth-century experience. It is enough to say that if Diderot, Adam Smith, and Jefferson had lived through what we have lived through, they could not possibly have believed in the friendly flow of history.

What, then, have we been left with?

We have been left, first, with the idea that progress is neither natural nor embedded in the structure of history; that is to say, it is not nature's business or history's. It is our business. No one believes, or perhaps ever will again, that history itself is moving inexorably toward a golden age. The idea that *we* must make our own future, bend history to our own will, is, of course, frightening and captures the sense of Nietzsche's ominous remark that God is dead. We have all become existentialists, which lays upon us responsibilities that once were shared by God and history.

Perhaps because of such a psychic burden, we have held on to the idea of progress but in a form that no eighteenth-century philosopher or early-nineteenth-century heir of the Enlightenment would have embraced—could possibly have embraced: the idea that technological innovation is *synonymous* with moral, social, and psychic progress. It is as if the question of what makes us better is too heavy, too complex—even too absurd—for us to address. We have solved it by becoming reductionists; we will leave the matter to our machinery. "In the next millennium," Nicholas Negroponte tells us in his book *Being Digital,* "we will find that we are talking as much or more with machines than we are with humans. What seems to trouble people most is their own self-consciousness about talking to inanimate objects."[2] But while acknowledging our "self-consciousness," Negroponte is impatient with it. He envisions a time when we may speak to a doorknob or a toaster and predicts that, when we do, we will find the experience no more uncomfortable than talking to a telephone answering machine. He has nothing to say about how we may become different by talking to doorknobs (and has no clue about how talking to answering machines is far from comfort-

41

able). He is concerned only that we *adapt* to our technological future. He nowhere addresses the psychic or social meaning of adaptation. People are quite capable of adapting to all sorts of changes—soldiers adapt themselves to killing, children adapt themselves to being fatherless, women can adapt themselves to being abused. I have no doubt we can adapt ourselves to talking much more to machines than to people. But that is not an answer to anything. It is the beginning of a question; in fact, many questions. I shall fill the rest of this chapter with some of them. They are not, literally, questions asked by Enlightenment thinkers, who could not have even imagined the technologies we have invented. Jefferson, Paine, and Franklin were, of course, inventors, and it is fun to ponder what they might think about talking to doorknobs. Franklin, I imagine, would find it amusing; Jefferson and Paine rather useless. In that vein, I think of the questions that follow as a kind of "thought experiment," imagining that Diderot, Adam Smith, Voltaire, Rousseau, Ben Franklin, Lord Byron, and other Enlightenment figures are accompanying us on our heady journey to the twenty-first century. I have imagined, further, that they are advising us on our technology, both new and old. And I have imagined that we are paying attention.

The most obvious question to be asked about any new technology—for example, interactive television, virtual reality, the Internet, or, for that matter, doorknobs and toasters that "understand" human speech—is, *What is the problem to which this technology is the solution?*

This question needs to be asked because there are technologies that are employed—indeed, invented—to solve problems that no normal person would regard as significant. Of course, any technology can be marketed to create an illusion of significance, but an intelligent, aware person need not believe it. There are those in high places and with easy access to our collective ear who, in speaking of the information superhighway, stress that it will make possible five hundred or a thousand television stations. Are we not, then, obliged to ask, Is this a problem that most of us yearn to have solved; indeed, *need* to have solved? Do we believe that having access to forty or fifty stations, as we now do, is inadequate, that they are not sufficient to provide the information and amusement we require? Or let us take as another example talking to doorknobs so that they turn at the sound of our voice. What problem is solved here? Is it that turning a doorknob is a burden? Is it a question of making doorknobs less vulnerable to burglars? Is it simply a matter of celebrating our own technological genius?

I have been told that Bill Gates, whose fertile imagination never gives him or us a moment's rest, dreams of a technology that would make obsolete the task of locating and then sending recordings into action. One approaches the machinery and speaks the words "Frank Sinatra" or "Pavarotti" or, if you can imagine it, "The Spice Girls," and we hear them. May one ask, What is the problem solved by this? The answer, I am told, is speed. We are a people who measure our lives in seconds. Five seconds saved here, five seconds there, and at the end of the day, we have perhaps saved a minute. By year's end, we have saved over five hours. At death's door, we may allow ourselves a smile by gasping that we saved a month and a half, and no one will ask, But for what?

That question was, in fact, asked on another matter— whether or not the United States government should subsidize the manufacture of a supersonic jet. Both the British and the French had already built SSTs and a serious debate ensued in the halls of Congress and elsewhere as to whether or not Americans should have one of their own. And so, the question was asked, What is the problem to which the supersonic jet is the solution?

Building a Bridge to the 18th Century

The answer, it turned out, was that it takes six hours to go from New York to Los Angeles in a 747; with a supersonic jet it can be done in three. Most Americans, I am happy to say, did not think that this was a sufficiently serious problem to warrant such a heavy investment. Besides, some Americans asked, What would we do with the three hours that we saved? And their answer was: We would probably watch television. And so the suggestion was made that television sets be put on the 747s and thereby save billions of dollars.

I do not speak here against a thousand television stations, self-activating doorknobs, or even American SSTs. I speak only on behalf of the application of quiet reason to the fury of technological innovation. On the chance that you do not believe me, I pause for a moment to acknowledge that I have a reputation as being anti-technology; in fact, as being something of a neo-Luddite. People who have labeled me as such usually know nothing about the Luddites. If they did, they wouldn't use the term unless they meant to compliment me. In any case, to come to the point, I regard it as stupid to be anti-technology. That would be something like being anti-food. We need technology to live, as we need food to live. But, of course, if we eat too much food, or eat food that has no nutritional value, or eat food that is infected with disease, we turn a means of survival into its opposite. The same may be said of our technology. Not a single philosopher would dispute that technology may be life-enhancing or life-diminishing. Common sense commands us to ask, Which is it? Only a fool would blithely welcome any technology without having given serious thought to the question. May I suggest, then, that we be particularly alert when reading books which take a visionary and celebratory stand on technologies of the future. Even if such prophecies seem plausible—especially if they seem plausible—we are not required to be tyrannized by them; that is to say, we do not always have to go in the direction that some technology would take us. We have responsibilities to ourselves and our institutions that supersede our responsibilities to the potential of technology. Technology, as Paul Goodman once remarked, is a branch of moral philosophy, not of science; which suggests that advice that comes from people who have little or no philosophical perspective is likely to be arid, if not dangerous.

Having answered the question, What is the problem to which this technology is a solution?, it is wise to follow with the question, *Whose problem is it?*

In the case of the SSTs, the problem was largely a concern of movie stars, rock musicians, and corporate executives. It was hardly a problem that most people would regard as worth solving if it would cost them large amounts of money, or any money at all. Most technologies, of course, do solve *some* problem, but the problem may not be *everybody's* problem or even most people's problem. We need to be very careful in determining who will benefit from a technology and who will pay for it. They are not always the same people. This is not meant to say that because I will not benefit, I will therefore decline to support a technology that is of benefit to someone else. Not long ago, at a public event, I had occasion to make some fun over the prospect of consumers' investing money in doorknobs that would turn at the sound of a human voice. At the end of my talk, a woman approached me, and speaking softly so that only I could hear, told me of her son who is a paraplegic. Such a doorknob, she said, would be a blessing to him. Yes, of course. I had not thought of that. There are uses of technology that do not come easily to mind. Still, we ought to know who is benefiting and who is not. Which leads to a third question, connected to but somewhat broader than the second: *Which people and what institutions might be most seriously harmed by a technological solution?*

Building a Bridge to the 18th Century

This was the question, by the way, that gave rise to the Luddite movement in England during the years 1811 to 1818. The people we call Luddites were skilled manual workers in the garment industry at the time when mechanization was taking command and the factory system was being put into place. They knew perfectly well what advantages mechanization would bring to most people, but they saw with equal clarity how it would bring ruin to their own way of life, especially to their children who were being employed as virtual slave laborers in factories. They resisted technological change by the simplistic and useless expedient of smashing to bits industrial machinery, which they continued to do until they were imprisoned or killed by the British army. "Luddite" has thus come to mean a person who resists technological change in any way, and it is usually used as an insult. Why this is so is a bit puzzling, since only a fool doesn't know that new technologies always produce winners and losers, and there is nothing irrational about loser-resistance. Bill Gates, who is, of course, a winner, knows this, and because he is no fool, his propaganda continuously implies that computer technology can bring harm to no one. That is the way of winners: they want losers to be grateful and enthusiastic and, especially, to be unaware that they are losers. Let us take schoolteachers as an example of losers who are deluded into thinking they are winners. Will anyone disagree with the claim that we need more teachers and that we ought to pay more to those we have? Nonetheless, school boards are resistant to hiring more teachers and to paying them more, and complain continuously about a shortage of funds. This resistance and those complaints notwithstanding, the fact is that school boards are now preparing to spend, in the aggregate, billions of dollars to wire schools in order to accommodate computer technology, and for reasons that are by no means clear. There certainly does not exist compelling evidence that any manifestation of computer technology can do for children what good, well-paid, unburdened teachers can do.[3] So where is the outcry from teachers? They are losers in this deal, and serious losers. Here, for example, is an announcement of an insult to teachers, taken not so long ago (June 11, 1996) from the *Washington Post:*

> Maryland plans to connect every public school to the Internet this year, part of a $53 million effort to give students greater access to far-flung information via computers, Governor Parris N. Glendening announced yesterday. Despite mixed reviews by national analysts who have studied computer use in schools . . . the plan calls for each of Maryland's 1,262 public schools to have at least two computer terminals linked to the Internet before winter and for each classroom to have three to five such terminals within five years.

Governor Glendening, who was re-elected in 1998, called this a bold and big initiative and expected that tens of millions of additional dollars would be donated by private enterprise, so that the total expenditure would come close to $100 million. Here is his justification: "Accessing information is the first, vital step in understanding and ultimately improving the world we live in." Let us put aside the fact that, at best, this is a problematic claim and, at worst, arrant nonsense. Let us also put aside the fact that even if the governor's claim is true, American students already have an oversupply of sources of information and do not require a $100 million investment to be well-informed citizens. Putting all of that aside, can anyone doubt that the following hypothetical statement (I have just made it up) would be happier news and more rational for both teachers and students? "The state of

47

Building a Bridge to the 18th Century

Maryland intends to spend $100 million to increase the number of teachers in the state, to pay those we have more, and to reduce teaching loads. Governor Glendening said, 'This is a vital step toward assuring that our students will be given a more attentive, wholesome, and creative education.'" One might think most teachers would support such an investment, but we hear very little from them on that score. In fact, many teachers are thrilled by the thought of a $100 million investment in computer terminals. Bill Gates must love this sort of stupidity.

But let us say that we have found a technological solution to a problem that most people do have, that we have some notion of who will pay for it, and that we are aware of those who might possibly be harmed. And let us suppose further that there is a will and even an enthusiasm to move ahead with the project and to speak favorably of its prospects. We have, then, the following question to ask: *What new problems might be created because we have solved this problem?* The automobile solved some very important problems for most people, but in doing so, poisoned our air, choked our cities with traffic, and contributed toward the destruction of some of the beauty of our natural landscape. Antibiotics certainly solved some significant problems for almost all people, but in doing so, resulted in the weakening of what we call our immune systems. Television solved several important problems, but in solving them changed the nature of political discourse, led to a serious decline in literacy, and quite possibly made the traditional process of socializing children impossible.

It is doubtful that one can think of a single technology that did not generate new problems as a result of its having solved an *old* problem. Of course, it is sometimes very difficult to know what new problems will arise as a result of a technological solution. Benedictine monks invented the mechanical clock in the thirteenth century in order to be more precise in performing their canonical prayers, which they needed to do seven times a day. Had they known that the mechanical clock would eventually be used by merchants as a means of establishing a standardized workday and then a standardized product—that is, that the clock would be used as an instrument for making money instead of serving God—the monks might have decided that their sundials and water clocks were quite sufficient. Had Gutenberg foreseen that his printing press with movable type would lead to the breakup of the Holy Roman Catholic and Apostolic Church, he surely would have used his old wine press to make wine and not books. In the thirteenth century, perhaps it didn't matter so much if people lacked technological vision; perhaps not even in the fifteenth century. But in the twenty-first century, we can no longer afford to move into the future with our eyes tightly closed.

I find it hard to imagine that Franklin, Jefferson, Voltaire, or Tocqueville (yes, definitely Tocqueville) would fail to ask a question about what unpleasantness may arise from our solving an old problem. And it is not sufficient to say, I think, that all technological change results in unforeseen circumstances. That is certainly a truism. But what of *foreseeable* circumstances? Would they not come into view through serious discussion of the history of technological change, of the kinds of social and economic disruptions that new technologies point to? Would it not have been possible to foresee in 1947 the negative consequences of television for our politics or our children? And if such consequences seemed clear and sufficiently worrisome, would it not have been possible through social policy, political action, or education, to prepare for them and to reduce their severity? Or, to put it another way, was it inevitable that by 1995 American children would be watching 5,000 hours of television before entering the first grade, 19,000 hours by high school's end, and by age twenty would have seen 600,000 television commercials?

Building a Bridge to the 18th Century

It is helpful for us to remember that there were no technological determinists among Enlightenment thinkers. There were optimists and pessimists, but none without faith in our capacity to reason ourselves into a felicitous relationship with our own creations. Which, I think, would lead them to ask still another question: *What sort of people and institutions might acquire special economic and political power because of technological change?* This question needs to be asked because significant technological change always results in a realignment of power. This was the sort of question addressed by Adam Smith (in 1776) in his landmark book, *The Wealth of Nations*. In it, he provided a theory that gave conceptual relevance and credibility to the direction in which industry was pointing. Specifically, he justified the transformation from small-scale, personalized skilled labor to large-scale, impersonal mechanized production. Do we need a new theory to justify the movement from an industrial economy to an "information" economy? We know that new technologies make old jobs obsolete while they create new ones. But it is likely that obsolescence will far outstrip the creation of new jobs. Is it possible that with the aid of computer technology ten percent of the population will be able to do all the work a society requires? If so (or anything like that), what is to be done with the rest of the population? Adam Smith would have had no answer to that question, but it is necessary that we do.

Of course, we have to ask the question first. And I fear that we cannot expect even our most intelligent entrepreneurs to ask it. They are, after all, dazzled by the opportunities emerging from the exploitation of new technologies, and they are consumed with strategies for maximizing profits. As a consequence, they do not give much thought to large-scale cultural effects. We must keep in mind that our greatest radicals have always been our entrepreneurs. Morse, Bell, Edison, Sarnoff, Disney—these men created the twentieth century, as Bill Gates and others are creating the twenty-first. I do not know if much can be done to moderate the cultural changes that entrepreneurship will bring. But citizens ought to know about what is happening and keep an attentive eye on such people.

In her book *Release 2.0: A Design for Living in the Digital Age*, Esther Dyson tries to assure those who worry too much about the new electronic world that human nature will stay the same. Of course. If we mean by "human nature" our genetic structure or biological needs or fundamental emotions, no one has argued that technology will alter human nature (at least not by much). But human nature is not the issue. What is at issue are the changes that might occur in our psychic habits, our social relations, and, most certainly, our political institutions, especially electoral politics. Nothing is more obvious than that a new technology changes the structure of discourse. It does so by encouraging certain uses of the intellect, by favoring certain definitions of intelligence, and by demanding a certain kind of content. Ronald Reagan, for example, could not have been president were it not for the bias of television. This is a man who rarely spoke precisely and never eloquently (except perhaps when reading a speech written by someone else). And yet he was called The Great Communicator. Why? Because he was magic on television. His televised image projected a sense of authenticity, intimacy, and caring. It did not much matter if citizens agreed with what he said or understood what he said. This does not in itself suggest that he shouldn't have been president or that he did his job poorly. It is to say that television gives power to some while it deprives others. It is not human nature we worry about here but rather what part of our humanness will be nurtured by technology. I have often wondered how Abraham Lincoln would have fared on television. Because of the invention of photography in

Building a Bridge to the 18th Century

the 1840s, he was the first president to be the subject of continuous comment about his looks (ugly and ungainly, many said). Would it be too much to say that Americans must be eternally grateful for the absence of television when Lincoln made his run for the presidency? Or perhaps we might say that had television existed, no such person as Lincoln could have become a serious candidate for president.

The point is that we must consider whether or not (or to what degree) the bias of a new medium is relevant to the qualities we require of a politician. The twenty-seventh president of the United States—William Howard Taft—was fat, very fat, well in excess of 300 pounds. We may assume that this physical condition would make him an unsuitable candidate in our own time, when the imagery of television dominates our perceptions. We may ask if Franklin D. Roosevelt, crippled by polio in midlife, so that he could not stand unaided, would have been an acceptable candidate in the age of television. We may ask of a more recent candidate, Robert Dole, if his inability to project an easy amiability on television played a role in his defeat.

We may take some advice here from Karl Marx, who understood better than most the transforming power of media. In *The German Ideology*, he asked rhetorically, "Is the *Iliad* possible when the printing press, and even printing machines, exist? Is it not inevitable that with the emergence of the press, the singing and the telling and the muse cease; that is, that the conditions necessary for epic poetry disappear?"[4] Marx is saying here that the press was not merely a machine (as television and the computer are not) but a structure for discourse, which both rules out and insists upon certain kinds of content, certain kinds of personalities, and, inevitably, a certain kind of audience. He did not, himself, fully explore the matter. But we must take all this into serious account.

Along these lines, here is another question: *What changes in language are being enforced by new technologies, and what is being gained and lost by such changes?*

Think, for example, of how the words "community" and "conversation" are now employed by those who use the Internet. I have the impression that "community" is now used to mean, simply, people with similar interests, a considerable change from an older meaning: A community is made up of people who may not have similar interests but who must negotiate and resolve their differences for the sake of social harmony. Tocqueville used the phrase "an ethic of reciprocity" to delineate what is at the heart of community life. What has that to do with "a community" of Internet users? As for "conversation," two (or more) people typing messages to each other are engaged in an activity quite different from what is usually called a conversation. To call messages that lack the presence of the human voice and human faces a "conversation" seems odd to me.

Think of how television has changed the meaning of the phrase "political debate"; or the word "public"; or the phrase "participatory democracy." In his book *The Electronic Republic*, Lawrence Grossman argues that new technologies will make representative democracy obsolete because they will make it possible to have instant plebiscites on every issue. In this way, American voters will directly decide if we should join NAFTA or send troops to Bosnia or impeach the president. The Senate and the House of Representatives will be largely unnecessary. This, he says, is participatory democracy as it was in Athens in the fifth century B.C. I have no objection to borrowing a phrase from an older media environment in order to conceptualize a new development; we do it all the time. But it has its risks, and attention must be paid when it is done. To call a train an "iron horse," as we once did, may be picturesque, but it obscures the most significant differences between a train and a horse-and-buggy. To use the term an "electronic town-hall meeting" similarly obscures the difference between an eighteenth-century, face-to-face gathering of citizens and a packaged, televised pseudo-event. To use the term "distance learning" to refer to students and a teacher sending e-mail messages to each other may have some value, but it obscures the fact that the act of reading a book is the best example of distance learning possible, for reading not only triumphs over the limitations of space and co-presence but of time as well. As for participatory democracy, we would be hard-pressed to find any similarity whatever between politics as practiced by 5,000 homogeneous, well-educated, slaveholding Athenian men and 250 million heterogeneous Americans doing plebiscites every week; it is dangerous to allow language to lead us to believe otherwise. Of particular interest, I should think, is the effect technology has had on altering the meanings of such essential words as "truth," "law," "intelligence," and "fact."

It will, perhaps, occur to you that these questions are at different levels of abstraction, and, if taken seriously, would require different modes and activities of response. Some of these questions invite participation in political activity, and can only be dealt with as matters of public policy—for example, the action of the Federal Communications Commission in giving, free of charge, the digital spectrum to the four networks in return for the promise of high-definition television. This is a political matter and ought to make citizens wonder what problem was solved by this action and for whom, and who is the winner and who the loser in the arrangement. As previously mentioned, the question of what technologies our schools spend our money on ought to be worth a few minutes (that is to say, fifty hours) of taxpayers' time. The replacement of people by computer technology, the environmental effects of technology, the unrestricted bombard-ment of TV commercials—these are public matters that ought to be the focus of discussion among enlightened citizens.

But embedded in some of these questions are guidelines for individual decision-making. I suppose I cannot put myself for-ward as a model citizen of the digital age. In fact, there are many people who, when describing my response to the digital age, con-tinually use the word "dinosaur." I try to remind them that the dinosaurs survived for a hundred million years, mostly because, I would imagine, they remained impervious to change. Nonethe-less, I find it useful to ask of any technology that is marketed as indispensable, What problem does it solve for *me?* Will its advantages outweigh its disadvantages? Will it alter my habits and language, and if so, for better or for worse? My answers may not be yours, almost certainly are not yours. I write my books with pen and paper, because I have always done it that way and enjoy doing so. I do not have a computer. The Internet strikes me as a mere distraction. I do not have voice mail or call-waiting, both of which I regard as uncivil. I have access to a fax machine, but try to control my use of it. Snail mail is quite adequate for most of my correspondence, and I do not like the sense of urgency that faxes inevitably suggest. My car has cruise control, but I have never used it since I do not find keeping my foot on the gas pedal a problem.

You get the idea. I will use technology when I judge it to be in my favor to do so. I resist being used *by* it. In some cases I may have a moral objection. But in most instances, my objection is practical, and reason tells me to measure the results from that point of view. Reason also advises me to urge others to do the same. An example: When I began teaching at NYU, the available instruments of thought and teaching were primitive. Faculty and students could talk, could read, and could write. Their writing was done the way I am writing this chapter—with a pen and pad. Some used a typewriter, but it was not required. Conversations were almost always about ideas, rarely about the technologies used to communicate. After all, what can you say about a pen except that you've run out of ink? I do remember a conversation about whether a yellow pad was better than a white pad. But it didn't last very long, and was inconclusive. No one had heard of word processors, e-mail, the Internet, or voice mail. Occasionally, a teacher would show a movie, but you needed a technician to run the projector and the film always broke.

NYU now has much of the equipment included in the phrase "high tech." And so, an eighteenth-century dinosaur is entitled to ask, Are things better? I cannot make any judgments on the transformations, if any, technology has brought to the hard sciences. I am told they are impressive, but I know nothing about this. As for the social sciences, humanities, and social studies, here is what I have observed: The books professors write aren't any better than they used to be; their ideas are slightly less interesting; their conversations definitely less engaging; their teaching about the same. As for students, their writing is worse, and editing is an alien concept to them. Their talking is about the same, with perhaps a slight decline in grammatical propriety. I am told that they have more access to information, but if you ask them in what year American independence was proclaimed, most of them do not know, and surprisingly few can tell you which planet is the third from the sun. All in all, the advance in thought and teaching is about zero, with maybe a two- or three-yard loss.

It gives me no special pleasure to report these observations, because my university spends huge sums of money on high-tech equipment. Strangely, many professors seem to prefer that money be spent on technology instead of on salary increases. I don't know why this is so, but here is one possibility: There are always some professors who have run out of ideas, or didn't have any to begin with, and by spending their time talking about how their computers work, they can get by without their deficiency being noticed. I don't mean to be unkind, but I can think of no other reason.

Chapter Four

Language

A student of mine who had an inkling of what this chapter was to be about suggested, as a title for it, "Diderot, Not Derrida." I found the suggestion tempting, especially because I am quite sure that the professoriat has been requiring their students to read the wrong Frenchmen. But, as you see, I rejected the suggestion—for two reasons. Too cute, was one. But more important, I am not writing here *about* either man. Were I to have used this title, I would have intended their names only as metaphors of two different attitudes toward language. But there is a specificity to naming names that works against metaphorical meaning. Diderot is, in fact, only one of scores of Enlightenment writers whose attitude toward language I wish to contrast with "postmodern" attitudes, and Derrida is likewise only one of many associated with postmodern thought; so it is best to reject a misleading attempt at alliteration.

In any case, when I am done I hope it will be clear why the Enlightenment understanding of language is preferable to the postmodern, and in particular, is far more useful and healthy to carry with us into the future.

The period which is called "the Enlightenment"[1] is also called "the Age of Prose." This is not meant to say that prose was an invention of the Enlightenment. It is clear that what we would recognize as exposition predates the eighteenth century by several centuries. Some scholars attribute the first "newspaper," and therefore an early example of modern exposition, to the work of the Italian Pietro Aretino, who was born in 1451, only a few years before the invention of printing with movable type. Aretino saw earlier than anyone the value of the printing press as an instrument of publicity, and produced a regular series of anticlerical obscenities, libelous stories, public accusations, and personal opinion, all of which became part of our journalistic tradition and are to be found thriving in the present day. But most scholars point to the work of Michel de Montaigne as the first (if not that, the best) exemplar of the personal essay. Born in 1533, Montaigne invented a style, a form of address, and a persona by which a unique individual could, with assurance and directness, address the unseen living, as well as posterity. Competing with Montaigne as one of the earliest and most influential prose writers is the Englishman Francis Bacon, born in 1561, who used the essay form with powerful effect as propaganda for the importance of the scientific enterprise.

There are other outstanding examples of prose, especially in the seventeenth century, including the enduring essay *Areopagitica* (originally given as a speech in Parliament), by John Milton. But it is in the eighteenth century that a combination of developments encouraged the growth and refinement of a style of exposition which became a standard literary form. These developments include the growth of science, the standardization of vernacular languages (which followed the emergence of nation-states), the widespread use of printing and a concomitant growth of literacy, the decline of the influence of Latin, and the diminished authority of the Church and its rhetorical traditions.

Although I am not here concerned with it, the modern novel, it should be said, is, for the most part, a creation of the Enlightenment. I do not refer merely to storytelling in written form, an art that goes back at least to the Old Testament and the Babylonian *Gilgamesh* and was a feature of the Middle Ages as expressed in romances, ballads, and allegories. I refer to fictitious prose narratives, intricately plotted and concerned with the lives of believable characters; that is to say, *Robinson Crusoe*, which Daniel Defoe began writing in 1719. But if one wishes to quarrel about which was the first modern novel in the English language, any of the following could qualify: Samuel Richardson's *Pamela*, Henry Fielding's *The History of Tom Jones, a Foundling*, Laurence Sterne's *Tristram Shandy*, or Oliver Goldsmith's *The Vicar of Wakefield*, the most widely read novel of the eighteenth century.

The creation of fictional narrative prose is a significant event in literary history. But I am here rather concerned with a literary form of at least equal or greater import—what might be called, perhaps redundantly, expository prose. As with the novel, it is somewhat arbitrary to choose the first example of eighteenth-century exposition. The French and Germans can make impressive claims about this, but I choose, at least as a date worth remembering, March 1711, when the first issue of Joseph Addison's and Richard Steele's *The Spectator* was published. There were similar publications at earlier dates, including Steele's own *The Tatler*, but none that exceeded *The Spectator* in readership; Addison estimated that it was read by one out of every four Londoners. There followed soon after an outpouring of exposition unequaled, to the present day, in scope, profundity, style, and usefulness. Jonathan Swift comes immediately to mind, with his *Proposals for Correcting the English Tongue* (in 1712), along with Bernard Mandeville's *Free Thoughts on Religion* (in 1720). After this, the deluge: Defoe, Bolingbroke, Chesterfield, Berkeley, William Penn, Franklin, Voltaire, Hume, Samuel Johnson, Diderot, Montesquieu, Madison, D'Alembert, Condillac, Kant, Burke, Rousseau, Adam Smith, Paine, Jefferson, Bentham—all of whom, and dozens of others, used exposition to give form to their ideas.

You might notice that, with the exception of Franklin and, arguably, Jefferson, I have not included in the list above any "natural philosophers," i.e., scientists. (The word "scientist" was not used until the mid-nineteenth century.) But experimental science was largely an invention of the Enlightenment, and expository prose, written in vernacular languages, was the literary form most suited to its expression. The discoverer of the circulation of blood through the body, William Harvey, who died in 1657, was among the last of the great scientists who wrote in Latin. Almost all of his successors chose to write in their native tongue, at least at some point. Included among these are Newton, Vico, Hales, Pemberton, Linnaeus, Priestley, Leibniz, Watson, and Lavoisier.

The connection between the growth of experimental science—in medicine, chemistry, physiology, and physics—and expository prose is, as I have suggested, not merely coincidental. The scientific revolution in the eighteenth century was, as much as anything else, a revolution in language. One might even go so far as to say that Enlightenment philosophers, natural and otherwise, discovered a method of using language that provided a truer representation of reality than had previously been known. And it was done by defining "true representation" as propositions susceptible to verification. Propositional language is the heart of exposition, as is the assumption that there exists an intelligible world of non-words: that is to say, "reality." Exposition proceeds under the further assumption that propositions (the world of words) can describe reality (the world of non-words), and that when this is done with clarity, logic, and rigor, it is possible to uncover the structure of reality with enough approximation to understand how it works. These assumptions produced spectacular results in science and, of course, still do.

61

Building a Bridge to the 18th Century

This point of view about the power of language to map reality, sometimes referred to as "British Empiricism," had its roots in the thought of John Locke and Thomas Hobbes, both of whom were committed to the language and doctrines of the new physical sciences, trusting that a way had been found to make reality intelligible and compatible with ordinary common sense. Not all Enlightenment philosophers agreed, most notably George Berkeley and David Hume, both of whom addressed the question of how words and other symbols relate to the world of things. Berkeley is notorious for concluding that matter does not exist, that in fact nothing exists except spiritual activity. Hume is known to all who took Philosophy 101 as having shown that induction is an illusion, deriving its force from a psychological intuition rather than a logical imperative. He taught that a priori truths originate in our own habits of using words, and give no information about the world. Propositions, he argued, are either certain and uninformative, or informative and not certain.[2]

The sentences above summarizing Berkeley and Hume are, of course, shameful simplifications, all the more so because Berkeley and Hume are famous, in part, for the clarity and elegance of their writing. I put the sentences forward only to suggest that the epistemology of eighteenth-century science did not pass without serious examination from eighteenth-century philosophers. Hume, for example, believed, as did many of his contemporaries, that deduction is the only form of true reasoning, which led him inevitably to his startling conclusion that inferences about cause and effect are merely products of our "imagination." The scientists of the age were not unmindful of the philosophical critiques of their assumptions but proceeded with their remarkable work nonetheless. One is reminded here of Zeno's famous paradox—his Talmudic "proof" that an arrow shot at a tree will, in principle, never reach its destination (my example, not Zeno's). Deductive logic is on Zeno's side. Reality is against him. Which is to say that inductive science may fail the test of deductive rigor. But that is the only test it fails.

It must be added here that Newton, Hales, Cavendish, Lavoisier, Priestley, and other scientists believed that the "truths" they uncovered were universal, that (to use the modern way of saying it) their truths transcended race, gender, nationality, and even time itself. They were strengthened in this belief by their use of mathematics, the structure of which coincided more precisely with the structure of reality. It must also be said that the best-known Enlightenment philosophers believed (anticipating Wittgenstein by two centuries) that philosophical indecisiveness and ambiguity arose because of muddled language, and that if such muddles were cleared away, philosophy would at long last be left with testable questions concerning human social life. They anticipated that there would arise a Newton of the social sciences, someone who, abjuring metaphysical language, could identify basic and answerable questions about the human condition. And thus a true merging of philosophy and science would result. This hope led to the idea that what we call today psychology, sociology, and anthropology would be scientific disciplines. In fact, there were several contenders for the title of the Newton of the Sciences of Man. Among them were Claude-Henri de Saint-Simon and Auguste Comte, who shared the beliefs that the natural sciences provide a method to unlock the secrets of both the human heart and the direction of social life, and that society can be rationally and humanely reorganized according to principles that social science will uncover.

We know now, of course, that their hope was unrealized, but we must not miss the point that its origin is in the faith the Enlightenment had in the powers of lucid language. And it is that faith that provided political and moral philosophers with the armor and courage to expose as false, nonverifiable, superstitious, and nonsensical a wide variety of hallowed beliefs.

I refer to those writers, many of whom I have already mentioned, whose essays not only defined what we mean by expository prose but in doing so provided a definition of what is meant by clear thinking. Diderot, Voltaire, Swift, Johnson, Rousseau, Madison, Tocqueville, Jefferson—they are to exposition what Defoe, Richardson, Fielding, Sterne, and Goldsmith are to the novel. Among the best of them was the scribe of the American revolution, Thomas Paine, who used the essay form to change "the sentiments of the people from dependence to independence and from the monarchical to the republican form of government."[3] His most widely read book, *Common Sense, Written by an Englishman*, was published on January 10, 1776, and by March of that year had sold more than 100,000 copies. No one knows how many copies were eventually printed but a fair estimate is 500,000. Since the American population at the time did not exceed three million, we can assume that one out of every six Americans bought a copy, and perhaps as many as half the population read the book. Some of Paine's other books were not as well received, particularly *The Age of Reason*, the manuscript of which he delivered to a friend in December 1793, as Paine was on his way to a French prison. The book is an assault on organized religion, and especially on the Bible.

I mention Paine and his work for several reasons, all of which may shed some light on what we may learn from the Age of Prose. The first is that although Paine was poor and had little formal education, no question has ever been raised, as it has with Shakespeare, about whether or not Paine was in fact the author of the works attributed to him. It is true that we know more of Paine's life than Shakespeare's (although not more of Paine's early period), but it is also true that Paine had less formal schooling than Shakespeare, and came from the lowest laboring class before he arrived in America. In spite of these disadvantages, Paine wrote political philosophy and polemics the equal in clarity and vitality (although not quantity) of Voltaire's, Rousseau's, and contemporary English philosophers', including Edmund Burke's. Yet no one asked the question, How could an unschooled stay-maker from England's impoverished class produce such stunning prose? From time to time Paine's lack of education was pointed out by his enemies (and he himself felt inferior because of this deficiency), but it was never doubted that such powers of written expression could be the possession of a common man.

Paine was not, of course, a professional philosopher. He had been a corset-maker in England, and then in America a printer. To write political philosophy did not require, of him or anyone else, the mastery of an arcane, specialized vocabulary. The language of the common person was deemed entirely suitable for the expression of philosophical ideas. In fact, there existed a certain prejudice against those who thought of themselves as professional writers, that is to say, those who had no other way of making a living. Rousseau, for example, suggests in *Emile* that the profession of author is an unnecessary (and even harmful) one, and in several places identifies himself as a music-copier by trade. Spinoza, who died in 1677, was a lens grinder to the end. Jonathan Swift was a cleric, Jefferson a lawyer and gentleman farmer, Lavoisier a scientist, Burke a politician. If one goes through the list of famous prose writers of the Enlightenment, one finds few who thought of themselves as professional authors; fewer, as philosophers; even fewer who made a living as either. These men were public intellectuals who had something to say to the public—not merely to one another—and who had found a form in which to say it. And that is why the consequences of their writing were so serious. Paine, as we know, found the words that made Americans revolutionaries (as Jefferson found the words that made America a country). Paine then turned his attention to France and, in *The Rights of Man*, found the words to justify the French revolution. For his trouble, especially for the clarity of his views, he was, at one point, sent to the Bastille by an ungrateful nation. When *The Age of Reason* was published, Paine was anathematized by the American public. Here, for example, is a short paragraph, among hundreds that could serve as well, which explains why:

> When also I am told that a woman called the Virgin Mary, said, or gave out, that she was with child without any cohabitation with a man, and that her betrothed husband, Joseph, said that an angel told him so, I have the right to believe them or not; such a circumstance required a much stronger evidence than their bare word for it; but we have not even this—for neither Joseph nor Mary wrote any such matter themselves; it is only reported by others that *they said so*—it is hearsay upon hearsay, and I do not choose to rest my belief upon such evidence.[4]

Bundled together in this paragraph is almost everything we mean by Enlightenment prose—the straightforwardness, the courage, the skepticism, the clarity. Is it any wonder that believers turned from him, and eventually removed him from the honor roll of Founding Fathers? Even some *on* the honor roll—Washington, Monroe, to an extent Jefferson—turned from Paine. Jefferson probably believed exactly as Paine did on these matters. But, after all, there are limits to reason and clarity.

I should add that Voltaire and Rousseau, among others, had to flee, at one time or another, from those whose anger was aroused by what they had written. Can anyone imagine that a philosophical tract written today would so infuriate the public, or even government officials, that its author would have to flee the country? It is hard to imagine this, not only because, in the West at least, we do not jail unpleasant writers, but also because both the interests and language of professional philosophers are too specialized and therefore too inaccessible. That is to say, who cares what they write? Who understands it?

The main point here is that Enlightenment essayists were popular; they were even famous or, in several cases, notorious. They employed a literary form which allowed them to address public issues. Their language and thought were rooted in epistemological assumptions about the relationship between words and things that led to scientific, political, and social progress. They saw their task as one of liberation, of bringing light, of relieving citizens of the burdens of prejudice, superstition, and ignorance; not of being granted the delights of tenure. And they came from a variety of fields. In Europe, they were naturalists, doctors, and ecclesiastics. In America, where Enlightenment ideas were put into practice on a large scale, most of them were lawyers. The authors of the Declaration of Independence and the Northwest Ordinance were lawyers. The American Constitution was drafted by lawyers. George Mason, who wrote Virginia's Bill of Rights, was a lawyer. So were Hamilton, John Jay, and John Adams. Indeed, for the first forty years of America's existence as a nation, all the presidents (excepting Washington), vice presidents, and secretaries of state were lawyers. Shall we say that the decline of lawyering as a learned profession is in itself a measure of the difference between the Enlightenment and our own age? Perhaps we should let that pass.

The assumptions about the relationship of language to truth that characterize Enlightenment prose, as well as the standards by which falsehood and nonsense can be exposed, were carried forward into the nineteenth century. Tocqueville, Thoreau, and John Stuart Mill wrote essays that will be read with profit as long as there are those who honor such assumptions and standards. My personal favorites are the speech given by Congressman Abraham Lincoln (in 1848) on why he opposed the Mexican War; the long essay by Emile Zola, "J'accuse," on the injustices of the Dreyfus affair (1898); and Mark Twain's "The Literary Offenses of Fenimore Cooper" (1895).

It would be foolish to say that prose writing of clarity, honesty, and power began to diminish in the twentieth century. In fact, there was more of it in the twentieth century than in the two preceding centuries. For one thing, essay-writing was accepted as the standard form in which to express ideas. For another, more writing was done in more media by more people. In the twentieth century, there have been more scientists, more social critics, more academics, more journalists than in all the previous centuries combined. Moreover, most people, that is to say, both writers and readers, have not in the least abandoned Enlightenment assumptions and standards about language. But this is not to say that the twentieth century has been free of threats, accusations, and doubts about such matters. It is my intention to describe what these are and to explain why, carried to extremes, they are an obstacle to clear thinking; that is to say, I want to discuss "postmodernism."

To begin with, the point of view commonly referred to as "postmodern" covers a vast terrain of cultural expression including architecture, art, film, dance, and music, as well as language. In the broadest sense, it argues that at some point in recent history (it is not clear exactly when) there occurred a striking and irreversible change in the way artists, philosophers, social critics, and even scientists thought about the world. And it is this change that takes the name of postmodernism (sometimes poststructuralism), because it calls into question some of the more significant "modern" assumptions about the world and how we may codify it—in other words, assumptions and ideas inherited from the Enlightenment.

In trying to comprehend more or less precisely what post-modernism is trying to teach us, I have found it near-impossible to locate two people who agree on what it is. Some say it is an attack on Marxism, some say an extension of it; some say it attacks Freudianism, others say it elaborates it. Some believe it to be radical in its sweep; some conservative. I have even found, to my astonishment, an essay in which I myself am put forward as a standard-brand postmodernist (and one of long standing), a designation which gave me a jolting sense of how Molière's eponymous character in *Le Bourgeois Gentilhomme* felt when he discovered he had been speaking prose all his life.

The fact that one cannot settle on a precise definition of post-modernism does not, in fact, mean very much. I suspect that in the year 1800 we would not have been able to get large agreement on what "the Enlightenment" meant. But I can avoid massive entanglements by limiting the scope of my interest to only two aspects of what appear to be features of a postmodern view. One concerns the role of language in human affairs, which I will address here. The other involves the question of "narrative," which I will turn to in a later chapter.

On the matter of language, I need to say at once that if a dramatic break occurred in our attitude toward language, it was not generated, announced, or promoted by modern French writers such as Jacques Derrida, Michel Foucault, Jacques Lacan, or Jean Baudrillard. Long before these names became familiar, the problematic nature of the relationship of language to reality became a focal point of interest to twentieth-century scholars, and especially to physicists such as Einstein, Bohr, Eddington, and

Heisenberg. In fact, Philipp Frank, one of Einstein's early biographers, observed that the theory of relativity was as much a revolution in language as in physics. Einstein struggled mightily with the force of conventional and habitual meanings, as for example of "time," "space," and "simultaneity." Like Humpty Dumpty in *Through the Looking Glass*, he knew that it is a matter of who will be the master of meaning, and in taking charge, he gave us his theory of relativity—the concept that time, mass, and length are not absolute but relative to speed and position. Einstein and his colleagues did not believe that words had "essential" meanings. They understood that language was a social convention and that both its structure and its content were not necessarily useful in understanding the nature of reality. In his book *The Meaning of Relativity*, Einstein wrote, "The only justification for our concepts and systems of concepts is that they serve to represent the complex of our experiences; beyond this they have no legitimacy."[5] Indeed, the idea that we are, in a sense, imprisoned in a house of language is concisely expressed in Werner Heisenberg's famous remark that we do not see nature as it is but only as a consequence of the questions we put to it. We might add to this J. B. S. Haldane's equally illuminating remark that the universe is not only stranger than we think but stranger than we *can* think.

To put it as simply as possible, it was well understood by physicists of the early twentieth century that language is *a major factor in producing our perceptions, judgments, knowledge, and institutions.* This point of view was certainly held and demonstrated, roughly at the same time, by anthropologists. From Bronislaw Malinowski to Clyde Kluckhohn to Weston LaBarre to Edward Sapir to Benjamin Lee Whorf, the role of language in the construction of reality (as the postmodernists would say) was well understood and was central to their work. Indeed, that is what Whorf's work was *all* about. And one may say something not far from that for many early-twentieth-century philosophers, including Charles Sanders Peirce, Anatol Rapoport, John Dewey, and Alfred Korzybski, the last of whom spent a lifetime explaining why language can never be taken to describe the totality of the world of non-words.

Starting approximately at the beginning of the twentieth century, almost every field of scholarship—including psychology, linguistics, sociology, and medicine—was infused with an understanding of the problematic relationship of language to reality. I most likely earned the title of "postmodernist" by pointing out how those in "media studies" took hold of the idea, especially Marshall McLuhan, whose famous slogan "the medium is the message" is as concise a summary of the idea as we are likely to get. I went, perhaps, to extremes by referring to the matter as the "Einstein-Heisenberg-Korzybski-Dewey-Sapir-Whorf-Wittgenstein-McLuhan-et al. hypothesis." For those readers who are especially interested in the "et al.," I have included, in Appendix II, a set of quotations from those of the past who accepted *in one degree or another* the view that language (as Wittgenstein put it) is not merely a vehicle of expression but also the driver. What it comes down to (or up to) is that we do not and cannot experience reality bare. We encounter it through a system of codes (language, mathematics, art). The codes themselves have a shape, a history, and a bias, all of which interpose themselves between what we see there and what is there to be seen. When McLuhan says, "the medium is the message," or when Tollison says, "we see things not as they are but as *we* are," or when Korzybski says, "whatever you say something is, it is not," they mean to call our attention to the role our codes play in our interpretations of reality. They mean to disabuse us of linguistic naïveté, to urge us to take into account *how* our codes do their work and enforce their authority. An example often used by

71

Alfred Korzybski to show the "invisible" bias of language concerns the use of the verb "to be" in English. When we say "John is stupid" or "Helen is smart," we speak as if "stupidity" and "smartness" are characteristics of John and Helen, when in fact they are words we use to indicate our *own* feelings. The sentence "John is stupid" is a shorthand version of something like this: "When I perceive John's behavior in a variety of contexts, I am disappointed or distressed or frustrated or disgusted." We are talking about ourselves here more than about John. But through a kind of grammatical alchemy the "I" has disappeared. Our grammar has forced us to "objectify" our feelings, to project them onto something outside of our skins. "Stupidity," in other words, is a grammatical category. It does not exist in "nature." Yet we imagine that it does because our language has put it there. If there are languages (as there are) that do not feature in their grammar the "*is* of projection," then this "mistake" will not occur. But other "mistakes" will, since the grammar of every language represents a unique way of perceiving reality. Yes, we do live in a house of language. We try to assess what is outside the house from a more or less fixed position within it. However, the house is "oddly" shaped (and no one knows precisely what a "normal" shape would be). There is a limited number of windows. The windows are tinted and are at odd angles. We have no choice but to see what the structure of the house allows us to see.

If in saying all this, I am to be called a postmodernist, so be it. But now I must add some reflections which will either consign me to the margins or expel me from the club altogether. The first is that much of what I have been saying about the relationship of language to reality was well known by Enlightenment thinkers—indeed, well known long before the Enlightenment. Plato said: "When the mind is thinking, it is talking to itself." In *The Tem-*

pest, Caliban says to Prospero: "You taught me language; and my profit on't / is, I know how to curse. The red plague rid you / for learning me your language." (Shakespeare also wrote: "A rose by any name / Would smell as sweet," which is true. But it is also true that a rose by any name—say, "garbage weed"—would smell quite different, as any advertising executive knows.) Thomas Hobbes, in *Leviathan*, said: "Understanding is nothing else than conception caused by speech." And, as we move closer to the eighteenth century, we find John Locke saying in his *Essay Concerning Human Understanding*: "Knowledge . . . has greater connexion with words than is commonly suspected."

Enlightenment philosophers suspected plenty. It would be something of a chore to find a writer of that period who had nothing to say about the connections between language and thought, and between thought and reality. Kant, Hume, and Berkeley wrote, one might say, about little else. Johann Georg Hamann believed he had discovered that language and thought are not two processes but one, and that those who think they are studying categories of reality are only studying means of human expression; that is to say, the medium is the message. Diderot was, among other things, a grammarian who wrote essays on linguistics and knew well how languages work their alchemy. Swift wrote a great deal about language; the pitfalls and peculiarities of language are, in fact, a dominant theme of *Gulliver's Travels*. The Marquis de Condorcet, a mathematician by training and skeptical of the powers of ordinary language, believed that the use of mathematical probabilities could lead to rational progress. D'Alembert, who was a man of letters as well as France's most distinguished mathematician, wrote thoughtfully about the differences between these "codes." Even Tom Paine, whose rapid-fire prose gave him little time to reflect on these matters, did pause once in a while to address the problem of language. How, he wondered in *The Age of Reason,* could Jesus Christ make anything known to the people of all nations?

> He could speak but one language, which was Hebrew, and there are in the world several hundred languages. Scarcely any two nations speak the same language, or understand each other; and as to translations, every man who knows anything of languages knows that it is impossible to translate from one language into another, not only without losing a great part of the original, but frequently mistaking the sense. . . .[6]

The point here is that the relationship of language to thought and reality, which is a preoccupation of postmodernism, does not represent a break with the past. It is, in fact, a continuation of Enlightenment thought, reinvigorated at the beginning of the twentieth century and kept in focus to the present day. But here is a significant difference between "then" and "now": With very few exceptions, Enlightenment philosophers did not doubt that language was capable of mapping reality. Many were skeptical— were aware of a multitude of linguistic traps—but that the world of non-words could be represented with approximate verisimilitude by words was implicit in almost everything they wrote. The idea that certain ways of seeing and categorizing are products of language habits was not unknown to them, but they believed that language, nonetheless, was capable of expressing transcendent "truths." It is in this respect that some postmodern thought separates itself from Enlightenment thought. Here, for example, is a passage in which a modern author tries to explain what is meant by "the social construction of reality":

... words are not mirrorlike reflections of reality, but expressions of group convention. Various social groups possess vocabularies, or ways of putting things, and these vocabularies reflect or defend their values, politics, and ways of life. For participants in such groups, these forms of talking (or writing) take on a local reality. They seem totally convincing. Yet their very "reality" is their danger, for each renders the believer heroic and the nonbeliever a fool. This is not to say that modern medicine is no better than witchcraft; by contemporary Western conventions it surely is. However, the words employed by physicians are not thereby rendered *truer* (in the sense of more accurate depictions) than their exotic counterparts. To possess an effective procedure, according to certain definitions, does not render "true" or "objective" the words employed in carrying out the procedure.[7]

This is a form of radical relativism that would have befuddled many Enlightenment thinkers. If I may be permitted another "thought experiment," I can imagine a synoptic reply by the advocates of reason that would go like this: "There are words that do not seem to refer to anything in the world of non-words. And there are 'truths' that cannot be verified, and which gain their authority from other words that cannot be verified. But many words *are* reflections of reality. To be sure, the reflections are at varying levels of abstraction, e.g., 'tree' is more abstract than 'oak,' which is more abstract than 'this eight-foot oak which you are leaning against.' But it is the key to intelligence, if not sanity, to be able to assess with some accuracy the extent to which words refer to the world of non-words. Modern medicine is better than witchcraft precisely because its language is a more accurate depiction of the world of non-words. 'More accurate' means closer to reality; that is, 'truer' or 'more objective.' You may say, if you wish, that all reality is a social construction, but you cannot deny that some constructions are 'truer' than others. They are not 'truer' because they are privileged; they are privileged because they are 'truer.' As for procedures that are effective, e.g., inoculations against smallpox, sending astronauts to the moon and returning them safely to Earth, and two hundred million other procedures executed daily by sane people, they work because they are derived from sets of propositions whose 'truths' have been tested and shown to be in accord with our limited understanding of the structure of reality."

Nothing I have said above means to imply that there can be certainty about our knowledge. It is the quest for certainty that the best-known "postmodernist," Jacques Derrida, has found dangerous, and which he suggests is embedded in the Enlightenment tradition. He calls it "logocentrism." There is no doubt that there were some Enlightenment philosophers, inspired perhaps by Descartes, who can fairly be charged with believing in the possibility of certain knowledge. The most notorious expression of this is found in an essay by Pierre-Simon de Laplace published in 1814. He wrote:

A mind that in a given instance knew all the forces by which nature is animated and the position of all the bodies of which it is composed, if it were vast enough to include all these data within his analysis, could embrace in one single formula the movements of the largest bodies of the universe and of the smallest atoms; nothing would be uncertain for him; the future and the past would be equally before his eyes.[8]

76

There is, of course, no scientist today who believes this, and there were very few in the eighteenth century. Then, as now, the idea of certainty functions, for most, as a kind of metaphor, reflecting the thrill of discovering something that appears to be true for everyone at all times, e.g., that blood circulates through the body, that the Earth revolves around the sun, that the rights of human beings derive from God and nature, that the market is self-regulating. Enlightenment scientists and political and social philosophers wrote of these ideas "as if" they were immutable and universal. Some of these ideas, e.g., that human rights are derived from God and nature, are highly debatable, and led in the eighteenth century to arguments about the sources of the origin and authority of human rights. One need only read the quarrels between Edmund Burke and Tom Paine to get a sense of the status of such "truths." These quarrels continue to this day, and one may wish to argue that these "truths," if they are such, are applicable only to Western culture. The term "Eurocentric" is sometimes used (always as a pejorative) to suggest that such "truths" are limited in their scope, and, in fact, may be thought of as mere prejudices. Of course, if one does deny the universality of these "truths," one must explain why some of them—for example, "those who govern must do so by the will of the governed"— appeal to people all over the world, why even the most repressive regimes will call themselves "a people's democracy." Is it possible that there is at least a universal resonance to these ideas? To label an idea "Eurocentric" does not necessarily mean it does not have universal application. After all, the claim that the blood circulates through the body or that the speed of light is 186,000 miles per second is "Eurocentric," at least in origin. Are these "truths" mere prejudice or are we entitled to treat them as if they are universal and immutable?

Building a Bridge to the 18th Century

If postmodernism is simply skepticism elevated to the highest degree, we may give it muted applause. The applause must be muted because even skepticism requires nuance and balance. To say that all reality is a social construction is interesting, indeed provocative, but requires, nonetheless, that distinctions be made between what is an unprovable opinion and a testable fact. And if one wants to say that "a testable fact" is, itself, a social construction, a mere linguistic illusion, one is moving dangerously close to a kind of Zeno's paradox. One can use a thousand words, in French or any other language, to show that a belief is a product of habits of language—and graduate students by the carload can join in the fun—but blood still circulates through the body and the AIDS virus still makes people sick and the moon is not made of green cheese.

One may also say something like this about the "postmodern" view of texts. Roland Barthes is frequently cited as the originator of the announcement of "the death of the author." He is usually taken to mean that readers create their own meanings of a text irrespective of the author's intentions. Thus, the meanings of texts are always shifting and open to question, depending on what the reader does with the text. If this means that texts (including spoken words) may have multiple meanings, then the idea is a mere commonplace. But if it is taken to mean that there is no basis for privileging any meaning given to a text over any other meaning, then it is, of course, nonsense. You can "deconstruct" *Mein Kampf* until doomsday and it will not occur to you that the text is a paean of praise to the Jewish people. Unless, of course, you want to claim that the text can be read as irony, that Hitler is spoofing anti-Semitism. No one can stop you from doing this. No one can stop anyone from misreading anything or rationalizing anything or excusing anything. Derrida, with whom the word "deconstruction" is most commonly associated, gave a superb example of how one may choose to misread, in his defense of Paul de Man's pro-Nazi writings during the German occupation of Belgium. De Man is one of the founders of the postmodern school of "deconstructing" texts, and when his pro-Nazi articles were discovered after the war, he wrote a letter to Harvard's Society of Fellows explaining himself. In such a circumstance, it is convenient, to say the least, to represent the view that all meanings are indeterminate, that there can be no definitive interpretations of any text. In any case, de Man's letter was filled with ambiguities and even outright lies, about which Derrida commented: "Even if sometimes a minimum of protest stirs in me, I prefer, upon reflection, that he chose not to take it on himself to provoke, during his life, this spectacular and painful discussion. It would have taken his time and energy. He did not have very much and that would have deprived us of a part of his work."[9] As Anthony Julius puts it in describing the affair: Derrida is saying that telling the truth should be avoided because it is time-consuming.

Derrida, so far as I know, has not argued that *any* meaning can be attributed to a text, only that there are wider possibilities than are usually accepted or expected. Perhaps there are no postmodernists who argue that *any* meaning can be justified. But in surveying the work of well-known postmodernists, I find no clarity about—indeed, no interest in—the standards by which certain meanings may be excluded. The process of making meaning from a text involves as much withholding meanings as adding them, and knowing the rules that govern when it is appropriate to do either is at the core of reasonable interpretation. Derrida, in fact, knows this as well as anyone, since his famous analyses of the contradictions in the texts of Plato and Edmund Husserl, among others, are as good a demonstration of how to read deeply as any we have. But there are those who have taken the act of

79

postmodern reading and writing to the edge of absurdity, as in the case of The Great Postmodern Spoof of 1997. Alan Sokal, a physicist at New York University, submitted a long essay to the journal *Social Text,* noted for its commitment to postmodern thought. After the essay was published, Sokal revealed that it was complete gibberish from beginning to end. Not error-laden, not overstated, not even an exercise in fantasy. Gibberish. Apparently, this was not noticed by the editors of *Social Text,* or if it was, they felt that gibberish is as good as any other form of discourse. Sokal has continued his assault on postmodern writing by joining with John Bricmont, a Belgian physicist, in writing *Fashionable Nonsense,* a devastating critique of the writings of Régis Debray, Jacques Lacan, and Jean Baudrillard, among others. Of Baudrillard's theories about "multiple refraction in hyperspace," Sokal (in an interview with the *London Times*) said: "In physics, the word 'space' exists, as does hyperspace and refraction. But multiple refractions in hyperspace? . . . It appears to be scientific, but in fact it is as pompous as it is meaningless."[10]

Pomposity we can survive. But meaninglessness is another matter. Fortunately, most of us have not succumbed to the pleasures of meaningless language. We struggle as best we can to connect our words with the world of non-words. Or, at least, to use words that will resonate with the experiences of those whom we address. But one worries, nonetheless, that a generation of young people may become entangled in an academic fashion that will increase their difficulties in solving real problems—indeed, in facing them. Which is why, rather than their reading Derrida, they ought to read Diderot, or Voltaire, Rousseau, Swift, Madison, Condorcet, or many of the writers of the Enlightenment period who believed that, for all of the difficulties in mastering language, it is possible to say what you mean, to mean what you say, and to be silent when you have nothing to say. They believed that it is possible to use language to say things about the world that are true—true, meaning that they are testable and verifiable, that there is evidence for believing. Their belief in truth included statements about history and about social life, although they knew that such statements were less authoritative than those of a scientific nature. They believed in the capacity of lucid language to help them know when they had spoken truly or falsely. Above all, they believed that the purpose of language is to communicate ideas to oneself and to others. Why, at this point in history, so many Western philosophers are teaching that language is nothing but a snare and a delusion, that it serves only to falsify and obscure, is mysterious to me. Perhaps it comes as a consequence of our disappointments in the twentieth century. Perhaps some of our philosophers have been driven to a Caliban-like despair: "You taught me language and my profit on't is that I know how to kill and be cruel." If so, it is understandable but not acceptable. Can we go into the future believing that gibberish is as good as any other form of language?

Chapter Five

Information

You can search the indexes of a hundred books on the Enlightenment (I have almost done it), and you will not find a listing for "information." This is quite remarkable, since the eighteenth century generated a tumult of new information, along with new media through which information is communicated. The newspaper had its origin in the beginning of the century, and by century's end, had taken on its modern form. Every country in Europe—indeed, most cities—had its own periodical, many following the pattern of England's *Spectator*. Unlike in England, censorship remained a problem on the Continent, but not sufficiently serious to prevent the proliferation of a variety of journals—for instance, *Diario, Zeitung, Almanache, Journal des Sciences et Beaux Arts, Tagebuch*, and scores of others, including the famous *Patriot*, a product of the city of Hamburg. Their purpose, in general, was to create a cosmopolitan citizenship, informed about the best ideas and most recent knowledge of the time. The same purpose was pursued, especially in France, through the creation of *salons*—gatherings of aristocratic and middle-class people who shared ideas and new information in social settings. As the century progressed, *salons* were established in many places, becoming of particular importance in Germany, Austria, and England. In England, the tradition of the exclusively male club took on the function of the *salon*, as in the case of the Scriblerus Club, founded in 1714 and frequented by Swift, Pope, and Boling-broke. The *salons* served especially well as media through which information about foreign lands could be shared. Beginning with Columbus's explorations, many European nations pursued policies of colonization so that, by the eighteenth century, explorers, merchants, and clerics from many European nations had stories to tell of exotic customs and strange people. All the major ports of Africa and India were frequented if not controlled by Europeans, who were also settling in North America and in newly discovered lands. They returned with original perspectives and startling information, and when Voltaire wrote his *History of the World*, he could include a chapter on China, about which much was beginning to be known. An era of new information was opened—about geography, social life, agriculture, history, and, of course, science and technology, the last of which required the establishment of academies for research and teaching: the Royal Society, the Académie des Sciences, the German Academia Naturae Curiosorum, the Berlin Academy. The eighteenth century also introduced engineering schools, commercial schools for training businessmen in accounting and foreign languages, and medical and surgical colleges. Indeed, beginning with John Locke's essay *Some Thoughts Concerning Education*, there followed a flood of books on the subject of children and learning.

All of this was accompanied by an unprecedented spread of literacy which had begun slowly in the seventeenth century and then accelerated in the eighteenth. Rousseau is the only major figure of the Enlightenment who was skeptical of the importance of literacy. In *Emile*, he requires the young to read only one book, *Robinson Crusoe*, and that only in order to learn how to survive in primitive conditions. Everyone else regarded the ability to read as the key to the cultivation of social, political, and moral consciousness. The English settlers in America provide a clear example of the obsession with literacy that characterized the age. Literacy rates are notoriously difficult to assess, but there is sufficient evidence that between 1640 and 1700 the literacy rate for men in Massachusetts and Connecticut was somewhere between eighty-nine and ninety-five percent, quite probably the highest concentration of literate males to be found anywhere in the world at that time. (The literacy rate for women in those colonies is estimated to have run as high as sixty-two percent in the years 1681–1697.)[1]

The Bible, of course, was the central reading matter in all households, since these people were Protestants who shared Luther's belief that printing was "God's highest and extremest act of Grace, whereby the business of the Gospel is driven forward." Of course, the business of the Gospel may be driven forward in books other than the Bible, as, for example, in the famous *Bay Psalm Book*, printed in 1640 and generally regarded as America's first best-seller.[2] But it is not to be assumed that these people confined their reading to religious matters. Probate records indicate that sixty percent of the estates in Middlesex County between the years 1654 and 1699 contained books, all but eight percent of them including more than the Bible. In fact, between 1682 and 1685, Boston's leading bookseller imported 3,421 books from *one* English dealer, most of these nonreligious books. The meaning of this fact may be appreciated when one adds that these books were intended for consumption by approximately 75,000 people then living in the northern colonies.[3] The modern equivalent would be ten million books.

The settlers came to America as readers who believed that reading was as important in the New World as it was in the Old. From 1650 onward almost all New England towns passed laws requiring the maintenance of a "reading and writing" school, the large communities being required to maintain a grammar school as well. In all such laws, reference is made to Satan, whose evil designs, it was supposed, could be thwarted at every turn by education. But there were other reasons why education was required, as suggested by the following ditty, popular in the late seventeenth century:

From public schools shall general
knowledge flow,
For 'tis the people's sacred
right to know.

These people, in other words, had more than the subjection of Satan on their minds. Beginning in the seventeenth century, a great epistemological shift had taken place in which knowledge of every kind was transferred to, and made manifest through, the printed page. "More than any other device," Lewis Mumford wrote of this shift, "the printed book released people from the domination of the immediate and the local; . . . print made a greater impression than actual events. . . . To exist was to exist in print: the rest of the world tended gradually to become more shadowy. Learning became book-learning."[4] In light of this, we may assume that the schooling of the young was understood by the colonists not only as a moral duty but as an intellectual imperative. (The England from which they came was an island of schools. By 1660, for example, there were 444 schools in England, one school approximately every twelve miles.)

It is clear that growth in literacy was closely connected to schooling, which in turn was connected to the enormous proliferation of information. We may wonder, then, why the late seventeenth century and eighteenth century are not commonly referred to as the age of information. The answer, I think, is that the concept of "information" was different from what it is today.

Building a Bridge to the 18th Century

Information was not thought of as a commodity to be bought and sold. It had no separate existence, as it does in our age; specifically, it was not thought to be worthwhile unless it was embedded in a context, unless it gave shape, texture, or authority to a political, social, or scientific concept, which itself was required to fit into some world-view. No one was ridiculed more in the eighteenth century, especially by Jonathan Swift, than the pedant, the person who collected information without purpose, without connection to social life.

A useful way to understand the Enlightenment conception of information is to peruse the famous *Encyclopédie*, the prospectus of which was launched in 1750 by Diderot. Among its predecessors was Pierre Bayle's *Dictionnaire historique et critique*, published in 1697, which had as its purpose promoting the importance—in fact, the virtue—of skepticism. Diderot's *Encyclopédie* had a similar purpose, which is to say that information was to be the vehicle through which skepticism, as a world-view, was to be advanced. (According to Diderot's daughter, the last words she heard him speak, on the day before he died, were, "The first step toward philosophy is unbelief.")[5] This purpose was pursued in nearly every article that appeared in the *Encyclopédie*, including many of those that dealt with crafts, technology, and practical matters. Diderot wrote essays on cooking, on the art of whetting knives, on the reform of the alphabet, and on the different methods of catching fish worms. In most cases, these were what we would call today editorials. Diderot was, at heart, a revolutionary, and his conception of information was as a weapon of social and political change. The idea of information "for its own sake" was alien to him, as it was to all the Enlightenment philosophes. One can find something of the same utilitarian spirit in Voltaire's *History of the World* and even in Samuel Johnson's *Dictionary*. All lexicographers freely admit that, of necessity, they steal from one another, and Johnson is no exception. He mostly borrowed from Nathan Bailey's *An Universal Etymological English Dictionary*, generally regarded as the first English-language dictionary, published in 1721. But much more than Bailey, Johnson used his dictionary (published in 1755) as a vehicle to promote the stability of the English language. Most dictionaries today are *history* books, describing how words *have been* used. Johnson meant his dictionary to be a *law* book, asserting how words *ought* to be used. His purpose was to "purify" English. (He most likely was influenced by such enterprises as the French Academy, established for the preservation of the "purity" of French.) While Johnson did not deny that language changes, he left no doubt that he was against its doing so, and his dictionary represents, in a way, his protest. Johnson's dictionary was, in effect, a philosophy of language, and the information it contained had as its purpose the advancement of that philosophy.

What I am driving at is that it is hard to find a text of the Enlightenment that separates information from a specific purpose. All the newspapers of the age regarded information as a weapon. America's first paper, published in 1690, indicated that its purpose was to combat the spirit of lying which then prevailed in Boston (and, I am told, still does). One did not give information to make another "informed." One gave information to make another do something or feel something, and the doing and feeling were themselves part of a larger idea. Information was, in short, a rhetorical instrument, and this idea did not greatly change until the mid-nineteenth century.

The change in the meaning of information was largely generated by the invention of telegraphy and photography in the 1840s. Telegraphy, in particular, gave legitimacy to the idea of context-free information; that is, to the idea that the value of information need not be tied to any function it might serve in social and political life. It may exist by itself, as a means of satisfying curiosity and offering novelty. The telegraph made information into a commodity, a "thing," desirable in itself, separate from its possible uses or meaning. In the process, telegraphy made public discourse essentially incoherent. It brought into being a world of broken time and broken attention, to use Mumford's phrase. The principal strength of the telegraph was its capacity to move information, not collect it, explain it, or analyze it. Photography joined with telegraphy in re-creating our conception of information, since photography is preeminently a world of fact, not of dispute about facts or of conclusions to be drawn from them. The way in which the photograph records experience is fundamentally different from the way of language. Language makes sense only when it is presented as a sequence of propositions. Meaning is distorted when a word or sentence is, as we say, taken out of context. But a photograph does not require one. In fact, the point of photography is to isolate images from context, so as to make them visible in a different way. In a world of photographic images, Susan Sontag writes, "all borders . . . seem arbitrary. Anything can be separated, can be made discontinuous from anything else: All that is necessary is to frame the subject differently." She is remarking on the capacity of photographs to perform a peculiar kind of dismembering of reality, a wrenching of moments out of their contexts, and a juxtaposing of events and things that have no logical or historical connection with each other. Like telegraphy, photography re-creates the world as a series of idiosyncratic events. There is no beginning, middle, or end in a world of photographs, as there is none implied by telegraphy. The world is atomized. There is only a present, and it need not be part of any story that can be told.

Storyless information is an inheritance of the nineteenth century, not of the eighteenth. It emerged as a consequence of an extraordinarily successful effort to solve the problem of limitations in the speed with which information could be moved. In the early decades of the nineteenth century, messages could travel only as fast as a human being—about thirty-five miles per hour on a fast train. Moreover, the forms of information were largely confined to language, so that the forms of information were as limited as the speed of its movement. The problem addressed in the nineteenth century was how to get more information to more people, faster, and in more diverse forms. For 150 years, humanity has worked with stunning ingenuity to solve this problem. The good news is that we have. The bad news is that, in solving it, we have created another problem, never before experienced: information glut, information as garbage, information divorced from purpose and even meaning. As a consequence, there prevails among us what Langdon Winner calls "mythinformation"—no lisp intended. It is an almost religious conviction that at the root of our difficulties—social, political, ecological, psychological—is the fact that we do not have enough information. This, in spite of everyone's having access to books, newspapers, magazines, radios, television, movies, photographs, videos, CDs, billboards, telephones, junk mail, and, recently, the Internet. If I have left out some source of information, you can supply it. The point is that having successfully solved the problem of moving information continuously, rapidly, and in diverse forms, we do not know, for the most part, what to do with it or about it—except to continue into the twenty-first century trying to solve a nineteenth-century problem that has already been solved. This is sheer foolishness, as any eighteenth-century savant would surely tell us. If there are people starving in the world—and there are—it is not caused by insufficient information. If crime is rampant in the streets, it is not caused by insufficient information. If children are abused and wives are battered, that has nothing to do with

89

insufficient information. If our schools are not working and democratic principles are losing their force, that too has nothing to do with insufficient information. If we are plagued by such problems, it is because something else is missing. That is to say, several things are missing. And one of them is some way to put information in its place, to give it a useful epistemological frame.

In the eighteenth century, the newspaper provided such a frame, and, given the present information flood, it may be the only medium capable of doing something like that for our use in the century ahead. Unlike more recent information media, the newspaper has a tradition as a public trust; it is given special protection by the Constitution (at least in America). It is more connected to community life than other media and, for all the imperial entrepreneurs who own them, newspapers still have editors and reporters whose interests are not wholly driven by the market. What follows, then, is an idea—hardly new—based on the retrieval of once useful definitions of and distinctions among information, knowledge, and wisdom. It is a proposal for redefining the place of information so that there might be at least one medium whose purpose is to help twenty-first-century citizens make sense of the world.

I should like to start the idea by referring to a cartoon that appeared some time ago in the *Los Angeles Times*. The cartoon is about an amazing new product that has just come on the market. The product is designed to be better than any computer or anything that one could use a computer for, including the Internet and web pages. The product is called a daily newspaper. And here are some of its selling points: It requires no batteries or wires; no maintenance contract is needed; it is lightweight, recyclable, and biodegradable; it is absolutely portable and will go with you on trains, buses, cars, airplanes, and even to bed; it is completely quiet, does not oink, buzz, or beep; no secret numbers, access codes, or modems are needed and it does not affect your telephone lines; one has unlimited use of it for about twenty dollars a month; it comes pre-edited for pornography, fraud, and typos; it requires no furniture space; and, last but not least, the product does not in any way contribute to the bank account of Bill Gates.

The cartoon makes a case for the importance of newspapers and for the reasons we may hope they will survive. But the cartoon largely concerns the *form* of newspapers and, except for the reference to the fact that the newspaper comes pre-edited for pornography, fraud, and typos, there is nothing suggested about the uniqueness of the *content* of newspapers. Perhaps this was omitted because the cartoonist assumed that the function of newspapers is to provide people with information; and when it comes to the distribution of information, computer technology can do it better than newspapers—that is, can do it faster, more voluminously, and more conveniently. In other words, if you want to promote the value of newspapers these days, perhaps it is best to avoid talking about information since the new technologies, including television, appear to be largely in charge of handling that.

Which brings us to the question: What is information and how much of it do people need? Obviously, information is not the same thing as knowledge, and it is certainly not anything close to what one might mean by wisdom. Information consists of statements about the facts of the world. There are, of course, an uncountable number of facts in the world. Facts are transformed into information only when we take note of them and speak of them, or, in the case of newspapers, write about them. By this definition, facts cannot be wrong. They are what they are. Statements about facts—that is, information—can be wrong, and often are. Thus, to say that we live in an unprecedented age of information is merely to say that we have available more statements about the world than we have ever had. This means, among other things, that we have available more *erroneous* statements than we have ever had. Has anyone been discussing the matter of how we can distinguish between what is true and what is false? Aside from schools, which are supposed to attend to the matter but largely ignore it, is there any institution or medium that is concerned with the problem of misinformation? Those who speak enthusiastically of the great volume of statements about the world available on the Internet do not usually address how we may distinguish the true from the false. By its nature, the Internet can have no interest in such a distinction. It is not a "truth" medium; it is an information medium. But in theory, at least, newspapers do have such an interest, and there are no editors anywhere who will claim that it is not their business to separate the true from the false. In fact, there is no problem older than this—how to know the difference between true and false statements. When Cain is asked where his brother is and he pretends not to know, God knows that he knows; indeed, he knew in advance that Cain would speak falsely. But for the rest of us the matter is not so simple. It is not my intention here to address the issue, although I will try in a later chapter. Here, I am addressing a problem no culture has faced before—the problem of what to do with too much information. One answer, of course, is to make oneself inaccessible to it. Some people do this, I among them. As I have mentioned, I do not have e-mail, to take only one example, because it would make me the target of carloads of messages, almost all of which have no fundamental bearing on my life. I have developed other means of withdrawal, as have many people, although it is not easy to do this. In America, especially, one is thought to be peculiar, if not worse, if one sidesteps the onrush of information. But I am not here concerned with individual strategies, some of which I have suggested in an earlier chapter. My focus here is on how at least one medium—the newspaper—can assist in helping everyone overcome information glut.

To say it simply, newspapers should, for a start, get out of the information business and into the knowledge business. What do I mean by "knowledge"? I define knowledge as organized information—information that is embedded in some context; information that has a purpose, that leads one to seek further information in order to understand something about the world. Without organized information, we may know something *of* the world, but very little *about* it. When one has knowledge, one knows how to make sense of information, knows how to relate information to one's life, and, especially, knows when information is irrelevant.

It is fairly obvious that some newspaper editors are aware of the distinction between information and knowledge, but not nearly enough of them. There are newspapers whose editors do not yet grasp that in a technological world, information is a problem, not a solution. They will tell us of things we already know about and will give little or no space to providing a sense of context or coherence. Let us suppose, for example, that a fourteen-year-old Palestinian boy hurls a Molotov cocktail at two eighteen-year-old Israeli soldiers in Jerusalem. The explosion knocks one of the soldiers down and damages his left eye. The other soldier, terrified, fires a shot at the Palestinian that kills him instantly. The injured soldier loses the sight of his eye. All of this we learn of on television or from radio; the next day we are told about it again in the newspaper. Why? The newspaper will add nothing, unless it can tell something about the meaning of the event, including why this event is in the newspaper at all. There are at least forty wars presently going on someplace in the world, and we can assume that young people are being killed in all of them. Why do I need to know about *this* event? Why is what happens in Jerusalem more important than what happens in Ghana? Will this event in Jerusalem have an effect on other events? Is this something that has happened many times before? Is it likely to happen again? Is someone to blame for what happened there? In this context, what do we mean by "blame"?

A newspaper that does not answer these questions is useless. It is worse than useless. It contributes incoherence and confusion to minds that are already overloaded with information. After all, the next day someone will be killed in Bosnia, and the day after that, in Indonesia, and the day after that, someplace else. So what? If I were asked to say what is the worst thing about television news or radio news, I would say that it is just this: that there is no reason offered for why the information is there; no background; no connectedness to anything else; no point of view; no sense of what the audience is supposed to do with the information. It is as if the word "because" is entirely absent from the grammar of broadcast journalism. We are presented with a world of "and"s, not "because"s. This happened, *and* then this happened, *and* then something else happened. As things stand now, at least in America, television and radio are media for information junkies, not for people interested in "because"s. I might pause here to remark that it is one of the most crucial functions of social institutions—the church, the courts, the schools, political parties, families—to provide us with the "because"s; that is, help us to know why information is important or irrelevant, socially acceptable or blasphemous, conventional or weird, even true or false. Some of these institutions do not do this work with as much conviction as they once did, which makes it especially necessary that a knowledge medium be available. And there is no more fundamental requirement of a knowledge medium than that it make clear why we are being given information. If we do not know that, we know nothing worth knowing. But there is something else the newspapers must do for us in a technological age, and it has to do with the word "wisdom." I wish to suggest that it is time for newspapers to begin thinking of themselves as being not merely in the knowledge business but in the wisdom business as well.

You may be inclined to think I am going too far. But I wish to define "wisdom" in a way that will make it appear to you entirely practical. I mean by wisdom the capacity to know what body of knowledge is relevant to the solution of significant problems. Knowledge, as I have said, is only organized information. It is self-contained, confined to a single system of information about the world. One can have a great deal of knowledge about the world but entirely lack wisdom. That is frequently the case with scientists, politicians, entrepreneurs, academics, even theologians. Let us take, for example, a story about cloning. It is mere information to tell us that scientists in Scotland have cloned a sheep and that some scientists in the United States claim to have cloned a monkey. We will be provided with knowledge if we are told how cloning is done, and how soon we may expect humans to be cloned, and even something about the history of attempts at cloning. But it would be wisdom to advise us on what system of knowledge we need in order to evaluate the act of cloning. Science itself can give us no help in this matter. Science can only tell us how it works. What can tell us whether or not we should be happy or sad about this? What can tell us if there are policies that need to be developed to control such a process? What can tell us if this is progress or regress? To begin to think about such questions, we would have to be referred to the body of knowledge we call religion, or the body of knowledge we call politics, or the body of knowledge we call sociology. Knowledge cannot judge itself. Knowledge must be judged by other knowledge, and therein lies the essence of wisdom. There are, I have learned, children starving in Somalia. What system of knowledge do I need to know in order to have some idea about how to solve this problem? I have learned that our oceans are polluted and the rain forests are being depleted. What systems of knowledge can help us to know how these problems might be solved? Or the problems of racism and sexism? Or the problem of crime?

If you are thinking that this sort of thing is accomplished in newspapers on the editorial page, I say it is not. Editorials merely tell us *what* to think. I am talking about telling us what we need to know in order to think. That is the difference between mere opinion and wisdom. It is also the difference between dogmatism and education. Any fool can have an opinion; to know what one needs to know to *have* an opinion is wisdom; which is another way of saying that wisdom means knowing what questions to ask about knowledge. I do not mean, of course, technical questions, which are easy. I mean questions that come from a world other than the world from which the knowledge comes. And nowhere is this kind of wisdom needed more than in the story of technology itself. That story—the changeover from industrial machinery to electronic impulse—hasn't been well covered by most newspapers, in part because most editors do not have a clue about what questions need asking about technology. They seem unaware that significant technological change always involves a re-ordering of our moral presuppositions, of social life, of psychic habits, of political practices.

The closest editors ever come to conveying a sense of the nontechnological meaning of technological change is in their speculations about economic consequences, which, I might say, they usually have wrong, mostly because they consult only with economists. But that is beside the point. Wisdom does not imply having the right answers. It implies only asking the right questions. Consider what most journalists might now do if given a chance to ask Bill Gates questions. What would they ask?—What is his latest project? How does his software work? How much money will he make? What mergers is he planning? I would probably ask him the same questions because, in fact, judging from his book, *The Road Ahead*, Gates may be the last person likely to have answers to the moral, psychological, and social questions that need to be asked about computer technology. Whom would we want to interview about *that*, and what would we ask? Consider who was interviewed by journalists during the U.S.-Iraqi war. On television and radio and in the press, generals, experts on weapons systems, and Pentagon officials dominated. No artists were interviewed—no historians, no novelists, no theologians, no schoolteachers, no doctors. Is war the business only of military experts? Is what they have to say about war the only perspective citizens need to have? I should think that weapons systems experts would be the last people to be interviewed on the matter of war. Perhaps the absence of any others may be accounted for by saying the first casualty of war is wisdom.

I can envision a future in which what I have been saying about wisdom will be commonplace in newspapers. I cannot envision exactly how this will be done, although I rather like imagining a time when, in addition to op-ed pages, we will have "wisdom pages," filled with relevant questions about the stories that have been covered, questions directed at those who offer different bodies of knowledge from those which the stories themselves confront. I can even imagine a time when the news will be organized, not according to the standard format of local, regional, national, and world news, but according to some other organizing principle—for example, the seven deadly sins of greed, lust, envy, and so on.

Do I ask too much of editors, too much of newspapers? Perhaps. But I say what I do because we live now in a world of too much information, confusing specialized knowledge, and too little wisdom. Journalists may think it is not their job to offer the wisdom. I say, Why not? Who can say where their responsibilities as journalists end?

This much we can say—and ought to: The problem to be solved in the twenty-first century is not how to *move* information, not the engineering of information. We solved that problem long ago. The problem is how to transform information into knowledge, and how to transform knowledge into wisdom. If we can solve that problem, all the rest will take care of itself.

Chapter Six

Narratives

The postmodernists do have a point, after all. The twenty-first century will be troubled by it if we cannot find a way around it. Among academics, it goes by the name of "radical historicism." To put it simply, which its advocates sometimes find hard to do, it is the claim that there are no ultimate truths, especially moral truths; that there is no transcendent authority to which we may appeal for a final answer to the question, Is this a right or wrong thing to do? What is the right thing to do, the argument goes, is determined by legislatures, courts, and churches, each of which is a human creation and has evolved over time so that its conceptions of what is right have changed depending on historical conditions. Moreover, different cultures have evolved different conceptions of moral rectitude, and there is no one who can say which culture has got it right. The Code of Hammurabi allows a father to cut off the hands of a son who strikes him, or to cut out the tongue of a son who says "You are not my father" to a man who adopted him; and permits a man to drown his wife if he has caught her being unfaithful. The Code also specifies that a physician who performs an operation that results in the death of a patient shall have his hands cut off. (Do we need to give some thought to this one?)

Can we say with certainty that the Babylonians were wrong on these matters? Some do say that, of course. Much of what is specified in the Code is disputed in the Talmud, which takes as primitive, if not barbaric, Hammurabi's morality. But much of what is in the Talmud is disputed by, let us say, the legislature of the state of Iowa. Who can say which of them is more moral? The legislature of the state of Iowa would claim that its moral world-view comes, authoritatively, from the instructions of the Son of God. Followers of the Talmud would say their moral view comes from the instructions of God Himself. The Babylonians found justification for their rules in the instructions of their own gods. To those who take their god or gods to be an ultimate moral authority, there is no problem. They clear their path by claiming that the gods of others are wrong. But to those who are in doubt about the existence of a god or gods, or about the nature of that existence, or about the claim that specific moral instructions come from that source, there *is* a problem. And such doubts were raised with great passion during the Enlightenment. The authority of religious systems was called into question repeatedly, and an alternative transcendent authority, Reason, was offered in its place. But as I have already discussed, Rousseau and his followers argued that, while reason may be useful in producing "scientific truths," it is the sketchiest of maps on which to base the quest for moral truth—indeed, is an impediment to that quest. In the nineteenth century, Nietzsche put the matter in a brutal light by arguing that reason is a kind of linguistic illusion, that good and evil are, equally, illusory, and that there is nothing but one's will and the power to realize one's will. In other words, there is no difference between the sentences "I want to do this" and "I have a right to do this." The second sentence is merely a disguise, an attempt to hide from oneself the naked expression of one's will.

Putting aside, for the moment, Nietzsche's uncompromising dismissal of (what some have called) the failed Enlightenment attempt to provide a logically unassailable basis for morality, it needs to be said that such figures as Locke, Hume, and Kant did make a serious effort to construct a secular, rational foundation for moral judgment, including a naturalistic conception of human nature. If one wishes to offer, as I do, a useful alternative to the Nietzschean and postmodern problem (there is no "solution" to it, only ways to ignore it), one will have need of a naturalistic foundation of morality.

But before we come to that, there are two ideas that need to be introduced. The first concerns the word that is the title of this chapter: "narratives." I mean by "narrative" a story. But not any kind of story. I refer to *big* stories—stories that are sufficiently profound and complex to offer explanations of the origins and future of a people; stories that construct ideals, prescribe rules of conduct, specify sources of authority, and, in doing all this, provide a sense of continuity and purpose. Joseph Campbell and Rollo May, among others, called such stories "myths." Marx had such stories in mind in referring to "ideologies." And Freud called them "illusions." No matter. What is important about narratives is that human beings cannot live without them. We are burdened with a kind of consciousness that insists on our having a purpose. Purposefulness requires a moral context, and moral context is what I mean by a narrative. The construction of narratives is, therefore, a major business of our species; certainly, no group of humans has ever been found that did not have a story that defined for them how they ought to behave and why. That is the reason why there is nothing more disconcerting, to put it mildly, than to have one's story mocked, contradicted, refuted, held in contempt, or made to appear trivial. To do so is to rob a people of their reason for being. And that is why no one loves a story-buster, at least not until a new story can be found. Much of our ancient history concerns the punishments inflicted on those who challenged existing narratives—Socrates was given hemlock,

John the Baptist lost his head, Jesus was crucified, Muhammad had to seek shelter in a cave. Even Moses, who fared better than most, was held in contempt by his own tribe, who thought the worship of golden calves had much to be said in its favor. In our era, the great story-busters—Darwin, Marx, Freud—were anything but lovable to the mass of people whose traditional narratives they attacked. I think I may say that even today there is nothing lovable about them, even to those who give credence to their arguments. Moreover, these story-busters have not had the effects they imagined, since old stories die hard. Darwin, I think, would be amazed to know how many people still believe that we are the children of God rather than of monkeys. Marx would be astounded at the staying power of the great narrative of nationalism. And Freud, who was sardonic about the future of an illusion and thought he had discovered that Moses was an Egyptian and not a Jew, would have to acknowledge that cold-hearted reason and meticulous scholarship are no substitutes for the great narrative of Genesis.

Nonetheless, beginning with the Enlightenment, skepticism about traditional narratives became commonplace, at least among intellectuals. Such skepticism had wide dominion, including implications for political life. The story about the divine right of kings was challenged. The story which gave authority to the practice of slavery was challenged. Even the story of science, especially its assumptions about the nature of truth, was challenged. As mentioned earlier, the great story-buster of science was David Hume, who was able to show that causality and inferential predictability are "illusions." Being a man of unusual calm and maturity, Hume did not expect, or even wish, his philosophical ruminations to overturn the scientific enterprise. As Thomas Haskell remarks, Hume "resigned himself to the imperfections of reason, shifted some of his trust to social custom and common

sense, and sought out convivial company for a game of backgam-
mon. Would that Nietzsche had done the same."[1]

Which brings me to the second idea. We think of Hume as a
philosopher—not as a philosophe, as we do of Diderot and
Voltaire. We may say that a philosopher is one who is devoted to
the search for truths that are both universal and timeless. We
expect such a person to be something of a recluse, like Hume,
and even more so, Kant. The term "philosophe" suggests something different. We think of a philosophe as a person who is
involved in political and social affairs, who is eager to change the
way things are, who is obsessed with the enlightenment of others.
As Henry Steele Commager put it: "The worst fate that could
befall a Philosophe would be exile or debarment from the drama
that so fascinated him: imagine Voltaire a recluse, imagine
Diderot silenced, imagine Franklin restricted to philosophical
speculations, or Tom Paine confined to one country!"[2]

The distinction between a philosopher and a philosophe is
worth making because it helps us to place the question of ultimate moral truth in a context; that is to say, it helps us to diminish the importance of the question. The philosophes were not
interested in intricate philosophical stories. They were interested
in practical, concrete matters as scientists, educators, humanitar-
ians, and reformers. They were against the Inquisition, slavery,
debtors' prisons, torture, tyranny. Although Kant's definition of
moral objectivity—"So act that the rule on which thou actest
would admit of being adopted as a law by all rational beings"—
(his categorical imperative) was useful, the philosophes did not
require it. The answers to the question, What is the right thing
to do? (or more precisely, What is the wrong thing to do?), were
"self-evident," based on the laws of nature that regulated "the
great machine" of the universe. It was Newton's discoveries
rather than Kant's ruminations that provided a narrative that

gave clarity and authority to their conception of moral, political, and social decency. And nowhere was this more explicitly the case than in America, which, we might say, was blessed with a paucity of philosophers. With the exception of Jonathan Edwards, who died in 1758, the American inheritors of the Enlightenment were philosophes, not philosophers. They were certainly not preoccupied with the mind and soul of the individual, or great theological and moral questions. They were concerned with society and its institutions. As Commager has remarked, the philosopher constructed systems; the philosophe formulated programs.

Among many others, Franklin, Jefferson, Mason, Madison, Adams, Dr. Benjamin Rush, Joel Barlow (to whom Paine, on his way to a French prison, entrusted the manuscript of *The Age of Reason*), Manasseh Cutler, Joseph Priestley (who fled England for America), and, of course, Tom Paine were America's answer to the great philosophes of Europe. Most of them were Deists, believed in progress (taking it for granted, they didn't bother to write about it much), practiced a conventional social morality, and created a country based on the principle of the "natural" rights of man. The phrase "the rights of man" was provided to Paine by Rush, but Paine added the subtitle (for Part 2), *Combining Principle and Practice*. Doing just that, in his book and elsewhere, Paine was among the first to speak against slavery. He also proposed a progressive income tax, bonuses for young married people, free schooling for the children of the poor, support for those thrown out of work, and freedom for working men to bargain with their employers. Although Rush had some curious ideas (for example, he believed the black skin of Negroes might be a form of leprosy), he argued against capital punishment and slavery, and believed women should be as well-educated as men. Cutler helped in the creation of the Northwest Ordinance, compiled a compendium of American law, and preached against the abomination of slavery. Franklin aided Jefferson in drafting the Declaration of Independence and, in a sense, made Philadelphia into the Athens of the New World. He believed that there could be no wisdom without freedom of thought and no liberty without freedom of speech. Of Jefferson, Adams, Mason, and Madison, enough is known of their ideas so that it is unnecessary to repeat them here except to note their hatred of tyranny in any form and their insistence on the freedom to worship whatever or whomever one may choose, or not to worship at all.

Where, in God's name, did these men get their ideas?

Some of their ideas did, in fact, derive their authority from God's name. Their narrative certainly included a divine principle. All of them—from Rush, who was a devout Christian, to Paine, who was hostile to traditional Christianity—believed in a Creator who intended humans to have inalienable and natural rights. The references to nature's God, the Creator, and Divine Providence in the Declaration of Independence are not mere rhetorical flourishes but a tribute to the ultimate source of authority in which all of the signers believed. But the Creator was not their only source of inspiration. The American philosophes were also inspired by their predecessors in Europe. The American Enlightenment came somewhat later than its European counterpart, some scholars dating its beginnings in 1741, with the founding of the American Philosophical Society. Moreover, it needs to be noted that the Americans were not as influenced by the French philosophes as by the British. We know of the American indebtedness to Locke and the British Empiricists for political guidance and inspiration. It needs also to be said that Locke insisted that tolerance for religious differences must be extended without distinction, even, as he put it, to "Papists." Hume poked fun at religion in general, and Roman Catholicism in particular, but opposed the "enthusiasms" (as he called it) that led people to favor suppression of religious expression. The Americans were also familiar with and influenced by the literature and history of Greece and Rome, especially Rome. George Washington was frequently compared to Cincinnatus, a Roman who left his farm to serve the Republic and then, relinquishing power, returned to his farm. Jefferson, in designing the University of Virginia, used Roman architectural traditions as a model. And, of course, those who contributed to the making of the Constitution rejected the Athenian idea of direct democracy in favor of the compromises of power in the Roman republic.

In other words, the ideas of the American philosophes were borrowed from a variety of sources—ancient and recent—to which was added a special dimension because of the unique geography and history of the "New World." William Cullen Bryant (in *Thanatopsis*) referred to the Founders as "patriarchs of the infant world." We may say of them that their ideas were the culmination and flowering of Enlightenment thought. America was the testing ground of a new narrative intended to provide practical answers to what is "right"—morally, socially, and politically.

We come, then, to the question: Exactly how can their narrative help us to manage things in the century ahead? There are several ways I should like to suggest. The first and most obvious is to reaffirm the necessity of a transcendent narrative, for without one, we can have no sense of purpose. Without a sense of purpose, we are left with only power as the source of authority. This is what Nietzsche and, I might add, Martin Heidegger failed to grasp. When they had finished their brilliant critiques of traditional narratives, what were they left with? Nietzsche spent his last ten years as a lunatic; Heidegger fell in love with Adolf Hitler. This is not a mistake the philosophes made. They proceeded with a narrative centered on skepticism, reason, and natural rights, to which they added the force of a divine principle. At the risk of vastly oversimplifying their story (and perhaps omitting some important details), here is my version of it:

"The universe was created by a benign and singular God who gave to human beings the intellect and inspiration to understand His creation (within limits), and the right to be free, to question human authority, and to govern themselves within the framework established by God and Nature. Humanity's purpose is to respect God's creation, to be humble in its awesome presence, and, with honesty toward and compassion for others, to seek ways to find happiness and peace."

I said a page or two earlier that this is the story in which the signers of the Declaration of Independence believed. In fact, one can say only that their public pronouncements would lead to that conclusion. It is possible, for example, that Jefferson and Franklin had doubts about the role or even the existence of a Divine Providence. (Ironically, I think Paine did not.) But, doubts or no, all of them proceeded *as if* there is a Divine Providence granting authority for their actions. They understood that vulgar relativism—that is to say, the idea that values are mere historical prejudices—would lead to despair and inaction. I do not think many of the philosophes would have disputed the use of different names for a transcendent authority. Natural Law, of course, was an acceptable term. But Practical Reason or First Principles or Traditional Morality might do as well. It was necessary to believe that slavery is wrong, tyranny is wrong, religious persecution is wrong, and that such wrongness transcends human opinion, or at least, confirms human opinion when it is guided by reason. They believed that, as there is a physical order to the universe, there is also a moral order, and that humanity is, and has always been, in a quest to discover its details. They believed that the human mind does not have the power to invent a new value, any more than we can invent a new universe. This view did not exclude the possibility of progress in the development of values. The philosophes knew that, in their own time, all people were not treated equally under the law (certainly not slaves and women), that freedom of speech was not fully protected, that religious freedom was restricted. Indeed, at the time of the federal Constitution, six states still had state-sponsored religious establishments, and some required an allegiance to Protestantism as a condition for holding public office. (State religious establishments continued in New England until the 1830s.) But the philosophes believed that, as science will gradually reveal our errors about the design of the universe and bring us closer to the truth, the maturing of our moral consciousness will do the same for our social life. Slavery would be extinguished. Freedom to speak one's mind would be increased and assured. State-imposed religion would fall.

We may ask ourselves, as we cross the bridge to the century ahead, if we believe in this story, and if we do not, what story *do* we believe in? And in answering these questions, we may include another: Does it matter if our story is "true"? In providing the world with a new narrative, Marx thought he had uncovered a true pattern of human social development: the inexorable movement of history toward the triumph of the working class. Darwin believed he, too, had uncovered a true pattern, that which governs the development of organic life: its evolution from simple and singular forms to complex and diverse forms. And Freud believed (or rather, hoped) that our illusions would be replaced by a "truer" grasp of our situation, that we would overcome our childish story of a superbeing before whom we humble ourselves, and from whom we derive our moral instructions.

It is possible that there may be some semblance of truth in Marx's tale. There is certainly persuasive evidence of the "truth" in Darwin's. And Freud's tale strikes rationalists as "true" in its rejection of a god who addresses humans, gives them instructions, and metes out punishments to transgressors. But here is a story that is truer than all of them. If it is truth we want, then let us hear Science itself speak of what it takes to be true: that

> man is the product of causes which had no prevision of the end they were achieving; that his origin, his growth, his hopes and fears, his loves and his beliefs, are but the outcome of accidental collocations of atoms; that no fire, no heroism, no intensity of thought and feeling, can preserve an individual life beyond the grave; that all the labours of the ages, all the devotion, all the inspiration, all the noonday brightness of human genius, are destined to extinction in the vast death of the solar system, and that the whole temple of Man's achievement must inevitably be buried beneath the débris of a universe in ruins—all these things, if not quite beyond dispute, are yet so nearly certain, that no philosophy which rejects them can hope to stand.[3]

Is this the story Freud hoped humanity's maturity would lead us to? Can we believe in such a story? I suppose we can in some corner of our brain, but it is the sort of belief we can do nothing with, and which does nothing for us—like some overheated postmodernist "believing" that blood circulating through the body is a mere social construction, or some philosopher of science "believing" that there is no logical basis for inferring that the sun will rise tomorrow, or some relic of Stoicism "believing" that nothing that moves will arrive at its destination. There is "truth" in such believing, but it is unusable. To do its work, a narrative does not have to be "true" in a scientific sense. There are many enduring narratives whose details include things that are not susceptible to verification. The purpose of a narrative is to give meaning to the world, not to describe it scientifically. The measure of a narrative's "truth" is in its consequences. Does it provide a sense of hope, ideals, personal identity, a basis for moral conduct, explanations of that which cannot be known? Albert Einstein knew as well as anyone that in the end all is buried beneath the debris of a universe in ruins. But it is not the story he used to give meaning to his life. He found another story, in, as he said, "a rapturous amazement at the harmony of natural law, which reveals an intelligence of such superiority that, compared with it, all the systematic thinking and acting of human beings is an utterly insignificant reflection."[4] This is as good a summary of what God tells Job as we are likely to find.

I do not say that Einstein believed in a god as the source of the moral beliefs of human beings. His references to God in other places ("God does not play dice with the Universe"; "God is mysterious but not malicious") may be taken to mean the "superior intelligence" he refers to in the sentence quoted above. Superior intelligence? What could he have meant? Perhaps he meant what Bertrand Russell meant when he said that if God exists, it is a differential equation. I rather think he did not, since his anthropomorphic reference to the order of the universe as reflecting a superior intelligence implies a kind of purpose that Russell's remark does not. In any case, I call attention to Einstein because he is such a clear twentieth-century exemplar of Enlightenment thought. And I connect him to John Stuart Mill, who is such a clear nineteenth-century exemplar of Enlightenment thought. Mill said: "The essence of religion is the strong and earnest direction of the emotions and desires toward an ideal object, recognized as of the highest excellence, and as rightfully paramount over all selfish objects of desire."[5]

What we may learn from these two great philosophes, Ein-

stein and Mill, is what they learned from their predecessors—
that it is necessary to live *as if* there is a transcendent authority.
"One can have the clearest and most complete knowledge of
what *is*," Einstein wrote, "and yet not be able to deduce from that
what *should* be the *goal* of our human aspirations. Objective
knowledge provides us with powerful instruments for the
achievement of certain ends, but the ultimate goal itself and the
longing to reach it must come from another source."[6] The other
source is religion. Neither Mill nor Einstein believed in the stories that give form and inspiration to traditional religious systems, what Mill called the "supernatural religions." But both
understood that we require a story that provides a basis for moral
conduct and has a transcendent character. They found it in "natural law," and in the capacities of "human nature." In their stories, human beings have innate feelings for the general good and
the unity of mankind. Mill called his story The Religion of
Humanity. Einstein spoke of Cosmic Religious feeling. And they
found the details of their moral code in sacred texts and history,
as well as custom; that is to say, in our obligations to those whom
we have judged to have acted in accord with the principles of
human solidarity. Mill wrote:

> . . . the thought that our dead parents or friends would
> have approved our conduct is a scarcely less powerful
> motive than the knowledge that our living ones do
> approve it; and the idea that Socrates, or Howard, or
> Washington, or Antonius, or Christ would have sympa-
> thized with us, or that we are attempting to do our part in
> the spirit in which they did theirs, has operated on the
> very best minds as a strong incentive to act up to their
> highest feelings and convictions.[7]

Building a Bridge to the 18th Century

That there is a tendency *as part of our nature* toward our being "moral"—detesting wanton killing, honoring parents, caring for children, speaking truthfully, loving mercy, overcoming egotism, and all the other exhortations we find shared by sacred texts—is a legacy of the Enlightenment. And that this tendency cannot be proven in a scientific manner but must be taken on faith is also a feature of that legacy. And that there can be no objection to one's believing in a divine source for one's moral grounding is yet another feature of the legacy, provided that one does not claim absolute certainty for one's belief. For it is clear that most Enlightenment philosophes understood that absolute certainty is an evil that chokes reason and perverts faith; is, in fact, the opposite of the religious spirit. They did not, therefore, find it necessary to have it "proved" that their narrative is certain, or superior to all others, or logically unassailable. Their narrative had only to be *sufficient* to guide them to a path of righteousness as defined by reason and historical agreement. The modern Christian apologist C. S. Lewis refers to "historical agreement" as the Tao, the summary of commands and prohibitions found in all collections of moral discourse from ancient Egypt to Babylonia to the Chinese analects to Homer's *Iliad* to the Old and New Testaments. The eighteenth century could not have used the term "Tao," but this is what eighteenth-century thinkers meant. This is what was "self-evident." And this is what provided courage and optimism.

It is commonly assumed that the twentieth century has brought about the dissolution of eighteenth-century narratives. It is clear that we have been recent witnesses, if not participants, in the rise and fall of three hideous stories, each of which claimed absolute certainty, each of which demeaned and then tried to eliminate other narratives, and each of which lasted long enough to produce unprecedented mass murder: Nazism, fascism, and communism. It is also assumed that, as we proceed into a post-

112

modern world, we are bereft of a narrative that can provide courage and optimism; that we are facing what Vaçlav Havel and others have called "a crisis in narrative." Old gods have fallen, either wounded or dead. New ones have been aborted. "We are looking," he said, "for new scientific recipes, new ideologies, new control systems, new institutions." In other words, we seek new narratives to provide us with "an elementary sense of justice, the ability to see things as others do, a sense of transcendental responsibility, archtypical wisdom, good taste, courage, compassion, and faith."[8] No one must underestimate the difficulties in this. We know that skepticism, disillusionment, alienation—and all the other words we use to describe a loss of meaning—have come to characterize our age, affecting every social institution. If nothing else, the almost worldwide return to "tribalism" signifies a search to recover a source of transcendent identity and values. We know—do we not?—how dangerous such searches can be, which is why no one need be surprised by the rise in the West of skinheads who have revived the symbols and programs of Nazism, or the emerging popularity in Russia of Vladimir Zhirinovsky, the "Russian Hitler," who promises the masses a future more fully articulated than a conversion to a market economy. Zhirinovsky takes his story from hell, but we must grant him this: He knows as well as anyone that people need narratives as much as food.

Where can we find such a narrative as Havel seeks? The answer, I think, is where we have always found new tales: in the older ones we have already been telling. We do not need to invent a story for our times out of nothing. Humans never do. Since consciousness began, we have been weaving our experience of ourselves and of our material world into accounts of it; and every generation has passed its ways of accounting on. And as new generations have encountered more and more of the world and its complexities, each generation has had to reread the stories of the past—not rejecting them, but revising and expanding their meaning to accommodate the new. The great revolutions and revelations of the human past, and I include the Christian revelation, have all been great retellings, new ways of narrating ancient truths to encompass a larger world.

We in the West are inheritors of two great and different tales. The more ancient, of course, is the one that starts by saying, "In the beginning, God." And the newer is the account of the world as science and reason give it. One is the tale of Genesis and Job, of Mark and Paul. The other is Euclid's tale, and Galileo's, Newton's, Darwin's. Both are great and stirring accounts of the universe and the human struggle within it. Both speak of human frailty and error, and of limits. Both may be told in such a way as to invoke our sense of stewardship, to sing of responsibility. Both contain the seeds of a narrative that is both hopeful and coherent. My two favorite statements on this matter were made 375 years apart. The first is by Galileo. He said, "The intention of the Holy Spirit is to teach how one goes to heaven, not how heaven goes." The second is by Pope John Paul II. He said, "Science can purify religion from error and superstition. Religion can purify science from idolatry and false absolutes."[9]

I take these men to mean what I would like to say. Science and religion will be hopeful, useful, and life-giving only if we learn to read them with new humility—*as tales*, as limited human renderings of the Truth. If we continue to read them, either science or scripture, as giving us Truth direct and final, then all their hope and promise turn to dust. Science read as universal truth, not a human telling, degenerates to technological enslavement and people flee it in despair. Scripture read as universal Truth, not a human telling, degenerates to . . . to what? To Inquisition, Jihad, Holocaust—and people flee it in despair. In either case, certainty abolishes hope, and robs us of renewal.

I believe we are living just now in a special moment in time, at one of those darkening moments when all around us is change and we cannot yet see which way to go. Our old ways of explaining ourselves to ourselves are not large enough to accommodate a world made paradoxically small by our technologies, yet larger than we can grasp. We cannot go back to simpler times and simpler tales—tales made by clans and tribes and nations when the world was large enough for each to pursue its separate evolution. There are no island continents in a world of electronic technologies, no places left to hide or to withdraw from the communities of women and men. We cannot make the world accept one tale—and that one our own—by chanting it louder than the rest or silencing those who are singing a different song. We must take to heart the sage remark of Niels Bohr, one of our century's greatest scientists. He said, "The opposite of a correct statement is an incorrect statement. The opposite of a profound truth is another profound truth." By this, he means that we require a larger reading of the human past, of our relations with each other and the universe and God, a retelling of our older tales to encompass many truths and to let us grow with change. We can only make the human tale larger by making ourselves a little smaller—by seeing that the vision each of us is granted is but a tiny fragment of a much greater Truth not given to mortals to know. It is the technology-god that promises, "Yes, you can . . . have it all." My own limited reading of Scripture tells me that that was never a promise made by God; what *is* promised is only that we should have such understanding as is *sufficient*—for each one, and for a time. For people who believe that promise, the challenge of retelling our tale for new and changing times is a test, not only of our wisdom but of our faith.

Chapter Seven

Children

Childhood was invented in the seventeenth century. In the eighteenth, it began to assume the form with which we are familiar. In the twentieth century, childhood began to unravel, and by the twenty-first, may be lost altogether—unless there is some serious interest in retaining it.

This summary of the rise and fall of childhood will strike some readers as startling, especially those who believe that where there are children (that is, small, young people), there must be childhood. But this is not so. Childhood is not a biological necessity but a social construction. I am always reluctant to use the much-abused phrase "social construction," but if it may be used at all, it applies to childhood. I once wrote a book describing the process by which the concept of childhood was formed, and here I will not burden either the reader or myself with an account of it. (In Appendix III, you will find a brief account, although somewhat longer than the first paragraph above.) But in this book, there needs to be something said of what happened about childhood in the eighteenth century. And the most accurate thing to say is that there emerged a theory of childhood—or, more precisely, theories. These became necessary because the eighteenth century was, as Lawrence Stone has expressed it, "a turning point in the recognition of childhood as a period with its own distinctive requirements."[1] Between 1750 and 1814, to take one example, there were produced 2,400 different titles of children's books. Before that time, almost none. To take another example, prior to the seventeenth century, the graves of children who had died in infancy or at an early age were not marked, which suggests that such children were not thought to have their own individuality. The practice of marking the graves of children who had lived even a few hours began spasmodically in the seventeenth century, and became commonplace in the eighteenth. Indeed, before the eighteenth century, it was a common practice to give a newborn child the same first name as an elder sibling, and this was still being done in the early eighteenth century. Edward Gibbon, born in 1737, explained why:

> ... so feeble was my constitution, so precarious my life, that in the baptism of my brothers, my father's prudence successively repeated my Christian name of Edward, that, in case of the departure of the eldest son, this patronymic appellation might still be perpetuated in the family.[2]

Nothing could be easier than to give examples of how, in the eighteenth century, the concept of childhood as a distinct stage of life took shape. This can be seen in the emergence of "children's" clothing, in the education designed specifically for children, in laws distinguishing children's crimes from adult crimes, in the games devised for children (in the mid-eighteenth century, jigsaw puzzles and travel games played with dice were invented), and in a more caring and solicitous attitude of parents toward their young. We can see this last shift in family portraits (by Reynolds, J. S. Copley, and others) in which the children are shown in easy and friendly relations with their parents, as against earlier portraits characterized by formal poses in which children look like deformed adults. Moreover, in the eighteenth century, the idea that the state had the right to act as a protector of children emerged with considerable force, so that gradually the total authority of parents was modified. Parents entered into a partnership with government in taking responsibility for child nurturing. And, of course, the act of flogging children and otherwise inflicting serious physical punishments on them came to be seen as unacceptable.

All of this and more was both stimulated by and a reflection of theories about childhood, two in particular. The earlier one is associated with the great English philosopher John Locke. His best-selling treatise *Some Thoughts Concerning Education* was published in 1693, and went through twenty-five editions in the eighteenth century. Locke did, by the way, approve of physical punishment in moderation but only until a child had developed powers of reasoning, after which psychological methods were to be used. Locke's arguments against physical abuse became conventional wisdom early in the eighteenth century, as noted by Jonathan Swift, writing in *The Spectator* in 1711.

But more significantly, Locke saw the connections between book learning and childhood, and proposed an education that, while it treated the child as a precious resource, nonetheless demanded rigorous attention to the child's intellectual development and capacity for self-control. In fact, Locke's enlightened views on the nurturing of physical growth had as their purpose the development of a child's powers of reason. A child must have a vigorous body, he wrote, "so that it may be able to obey and execute the orders of the *mind* [his italics]." Locke also grasped the importance of shame as a means of maintaining the distinction between childhood and adulthood. "Esteem and disgrace are, of all others," he wrote, "the most powerful incentives to the mind, when once it is brought to relish them. If you can get into children a love of credit, and an apprehension of shame and disgrace, you have . . . put into 'em the true principle."

But most of all, Locke furthered the theory of childhood through his well-known idea that at birth the mind is a blank tablet, a tabula rasa. Thus, a heavy responsibility fell to parents and schoolmasters (and then, later, to government) for what is eventually written on the mind. An ignorant, shameless, undisciplined child represented the failure of adults, not the child. Like Freud's ideas about psychic repression two hundred years later, Locke's tabula rasa created a sense of guilt in parents about their children's development, and provided the psychological grounds for making the careful nurturing of children a national priority, at least among the merchant classes, who were, so to speak, Locke's constituents. And although Locke was no Horace Mann, in that his imagination did not admit of equal schooling for all children, he did propose a program of apprenticeships for the education of poor children, whose minds, after all, were as malleable as those of the middle and upper classes.

A second great eighteenth-century intellectual influence on the idea of childhood was, of course, Rousseau. Although I believe Rousseau did not clearly understand why childhood had arisen and how it might be maintained (whereas Locke did), he made two powerful contributions to its development. The first was in his insistence that the child is important in himself, and not merely a means to an end. In this he differed sharply from Locke, who saw the child at every point as a potential citizen and perhaps merchant. Rousseau's idea was not entirely original, for at the time Rousseau was writing there already existed in France a certain reverence for the charm and value of childhood. Indeed, Rousseau himself quotes an old gentleman who, upon being asked by Louis XV whether he liked the eighteenth century better than the seventeenth, replied, "Sire, I spent my youth in reverence towards the old. I find myself compelled to spend my old age in reverence to the young." But Rousseau's power as a writer and his charismatic personality were so great that most of his followers even refused to believe, as Voltaire and other enemies of his revealed, that Rousseau had abandoned his own children to orphanages.

Still, whatever his personal shortcomings, Rousseau's writings aroused a curiosity about the nature of childhood that persists to the present day. We might fairly say that Friedrich Froebel, Johann Pestalozzi, Marie Montessori, Jean Piaget, Arnold Gesell, and A. S. Neill are all Rousseau's intellectual heirs. (Froebel and Pestalozzi explicitly proclaimed their debt.) Certainly their work proceeded from the assumption that the psychology of children is fundamentally different from that of adults, and is to be valued for itself.

Rousseau's second idea was that a child's intellectual and emotional life is important, not because we must know about it in order to teach and train our children, but because childhood is the stage of life when man most closely approximates the "state of nature." Rousseau valued such a state to a degree that no one has since approached, except, perhaps, Californians. As I have mentioned, in *Emile*, Rousseau allows only one book to be read by children: *Robinson Crusoe*. And this only because the book demonstrates how man may live in and control a "natural environment." Rousseau's obsession with a state of nature and his corresponding contempt for "civilized values" brought to the world's attention, as no one had done before him, the childhood virtues of spontaneity, purity, strength, and joy, all of which came to be seen as features to nurture and celebrate. And the great artists of the Romantic movement did not fail to take up the *joie de vivre* of childhood as a theme. Wordsworth's poetry in particular depicts adults as "fallen children" and celebrates childhood innocence and naturalness. Wagner's *Siegfried* is often cited as the most powerful expression of the virtues of adolescence. And it is in the eighteenth century, we should remember, that Gainsborough painted the most romantic and charming picture of adolescence that has ever been done, his *Blue Boy*.

And so as the concept of childhood moved into the nineteenth and twentieth centuries, and as it crossed the Atlantic to the New World, there were two intellectual strains of which the idea was composed. We might call them the Lockean, or the Protestant, conception of childhood, and the Rousseauian, or the Romantic, conception. In the Protestant view, the child is an unformed person who, through literacy, education, reason, self-control, and shame, may be made into a civilized adult. In the Romantic view, it is not the unformed child but the deformed adult who is the problem. The child possesses as his or her birthright capacities for candor, understanding, curiosity, and spontaneity that are deadened by literacy, education, reason, self-control, and shame.

The difference between these two views can be seen most vividly by attending to the contrasting metaphors of childhood put forward by Locke and Rousseau. I do not believe it has been much remarked, for example, that Locke's metaphor of the mind as a tablet depicts precisely the connection between childhood and the printed word. Indeed, the tabula rasa sees the child as an inadequately written book, advancing toward maturity as the pages are filled. There is nothing "natural" or biological about this process. It is a process of symbolic development—sequential, segmented, linguistic. To Locke and most eighteenth-century thinkers, illiteracy and childhood were inseparable, adulthood being defined as total linguistic competence.

On the other hand, Rousseau wrote in *Emile* that "plants are improved by cultivation, and man by education." Here is the child as a wild plant, which can hardly be improved by book learning. Its growth is organic and natural; childhood requires only that it not be suffocated by civilization's diseased outpourings. To Rousseau, education was essentially a subtraction process; to Locke, an addition process. But whatever the differences between these two metaphors, they do have in common a concern for the future. Locke wanted education to result in a rich, varied, and copious book; Rousseau wanted education to result in a healthy flower. This is important to keep in mind, for a concern for the future is increasingly missing from the metaphors of childhood in the present day. Neither Locke nor Rousseau ever doubted that childhood required the future-oriented guidance of adults.

In America, of course, the Protestant view dominated throughout much of the nineteenth century, although the Romantic view was never completely absent. Indeed, we might say that America's greatest book, *The Adventures of Huckleberry Finn*, published in 1884, presents the case for the Romantic view. Certainly Twain attacked the presumption that children are, in any but the most superficial sense, unformed. And he mocked the claim that their character may be vastly improved by society's "values." Huck's innate sense of fairness and dignity, his resourcefulness and psychological strength, his sheer *interest* in life—all of this struck a blow for the Romantic vision of childhood and was part of a general trend, beginning toward the end of the nineteenth century, of a reassessment of the nature of childhood.

At the end of the nineteenth century, the stage was set for two men whose work eventually established the mode of discourse to be used in all discussions of childhood in the twentieth century.

The most influential book of each man, in its way, led thoughtful people to pose the question: How do we balance the claims of civilization against the claims of a child's nature? I refer to Sigmund Freud's *The Interpretation of Dreams* and John Dewey's *The School and Society*. Both men and their work are too well known to require much explication, but this much must be said: Taken together, they represent a synthesis and summation of childhood's journey from the seventeenth century to the twentieth.

From within a framework of science, Freud claimed, first of all, that there is an undeniable structure, as well as a special content, to the mind of the child—e.g., that children possess sexuality and are imbued with complexes and instinctive psychological drives. He also claimed that in their efforts to achieve mature adulthood, children must overcome, outgrow, and sublimate their instinctual passions. Freud thus refutes Locke and confirms Rousseau: The mind is not a tabula rasa; the child's mind does approximate a "state of nature"; to some extent the demands of nature must be taken into account or permanent personality dysfunction will result. But at the same time, Freud refutes Rousseau and confirms Locke: The earliest interactions between child and parents are decisive in determining the kind of adult the child will be; through reason, the passions of the mind may be controlled; civilization is quite impossible without repression and sublimation.

In a similar way, although from a framework of philosophy, Dewey argued that the psychological needs of the child must be addressed in terms of what the child is, not what the child will be. At home and in school adults must ask, What does the child need *now*? What problems must he or she solve *now*? Only in this way, Dewey believed, will the child become a constructive participant in the social life of the community. "If we identify ourselves with the real instincts and needs of childhood," he wrote, "and [require] only [their] fullest assertion and growth . . . discipline and culture of adult life shall all come in their due season."[3]

Freud and Dewey crystallized the basic paradigm of childhood that had been forming since the printing press: the child as schoolboy or schoolgirl whose self and individuality must be preserved by nurturing, whose capacity for self-control, deferred gratification, and logical thought must be extended, whose knowledge of life must be under the control of adults. Yet at the same time, children are understood as having their own rules for development, and a charm, curiosity, and exuberance that must not be strangled—indeed, are strangled only at the risk of losing mature adulthood.

Freud and Dewey were writing at the end of the nineteenth century and the beginning of the twentieth. Dewey died in 1952, Freud in 1939, and neither anticipated—who did?—the later-twentieth-century conditions that would render eighteenth-century conceptions of childhood problematic. I refer, of course, to the "information revolution" which has made it impossible to keep secrets from the young—sexual secrets, political secrets, social secrets, historical secrets, medical secrets; that is to say, the full content of adult life, which must be kept at least partially hidden from the young if there is to be a category of life known as childhood.

There was no theory of childhood, at least after the invention of the printing press with movable type, that did not assume that the information environment of adults is different from the information environment of children, and that the former is fuller, richer, broader, and, to pay respects to Rousseau and life itself, more depressing and scary. The word "socialization" implies this. It means a process whereby the young are inducted gradually and in psychologically assimilable ways into the world of adulthood. But if the technology of a culture makes it impossible to conceal anything from the young, in what sense can we say childhood exists? Yes, as always, we have young, small people among us. But if, by seven or eight or even eleven and twelve, they have access to the same information as do adults, how do adults guide their future? What does a forty-year-old have to teach a twelve-year-old if both of them have been seeing the same TV programs, the same movies, the same advertisements, the same news shows, listening to the same CDs and calling forth the same information on the Internet?

The answer comes back to us in the form of another theory whose practical expression is easily seen in America. Children are neither blank tablets nor budding plants. They are markets; that is to say, consumers whose needs for products are roughly the same as the needs of adults. There may be some differences in the types of toys and other amusements adults and children are enticed to buy but, for that matter, there are differences between what one might sell to the rich and the poor, irrespective of age. The point is that childhood, if it can be said to exist at all, is now an economic category. There is very little the culture wants to do for children except to make them into consumers. A child is someone who has money to buy things. An adult is someone who has more money to buy things. That is why children as young as eleven and twelve have inflicted upon them what is called "career training," a clear symptom of the idea that they are merely miniature adults. And that is also why in thousands of American schools, students are now required to watch commercials on a daily basis.[4] Since children are required to attend school by law, we can say that this is the first time in the history of the world that children (or anybody else) are required *by law* to give their attention to the hawking of products. It is devoutly to be wished that some of the children do *not* actually give their attention to this, but in any case, it is astounding that the matter has not been widely discussed. On the other hand, why should it be? The whole idea of schooling, now, is to prepare the young for competent entry into the economic life of a community so that they will continue to be devoted consumers. To put a pseudo-religious dimension on it, we might say that the theory behind all of this argues that the surest way to earn God's favor is to buy things, and it doesn't matter how old you are.

In this conception, a child's mind is not the pages of a book, and a child is not a plant to be pruned. A child is an economic creature, not different from an adult, whose sense of worth is to be founded entirely on his or her capacity to secure material benefits, and whose purpose is to fuel a market economy. Not even Adam Smith would have wanted such a thing; nor Karl Marx. Of course, it should be said that there is nothing new in conceiving of children as having little else but economic value. This was certainly the case in the medieval world, when there were only two stages of life—infancy and adulthood. And throughout modern history, including the Enlightenment, there have been places, and there still are, where the labor of the young is all that was asked of them, all that was needed of them, all they could offer. But it was in the eighteenth century that a new conception of the young flourished. It took the name of "childhood," a third stage of life, delightful in itself, providing adults with the time and opportunity to create from it a mature and humane person. Do we leave this idea behind in crossing the bridge to the new millennium?

To those who say we must not, I address the following remarks, beginning with the question: Was childhood discovered or invented? I said at the start of this chapter that childhood was a social construction, which is to say, not a biological necessity; which is to say further, invented not discovered. But I could be wrong about this, and hope I am. Researchers such as Freud, Erik Erikson, Arnold Gesell, and, in particular, Jean Piaget, have held that observable stages of child development are governed by biological imperatives. Indeed, Piaget called his studies "genetic epistemology," by which he meant that the child's advance from one level of intellectual achievement to the next follows a genetic principle. If Piaget is right, then childhood was not invented by a dramatic change in the communication environment (i.e., the printing press) but only discovered, and the new information environment is not "disappearing" childhood but only suppressing it.

I believe Piaget's studies are limited by his essentially ahistorical approach. He gives insufficient attention to the possibility that the behaviors he observed in children might have been absent or at least quite different in earlier historical periods. Nonetheless, I rather hope that he is correct. If he is, we may encourage ourselves to believe that, given the slightest chance, childhood will assert itself, for, as it is said, you cannot fool Mother Nature, at least not forever. If, however, childhood is solely a creation of culture, as I am inclined to believe, then it would have to await a dramatic restructuring of our communication environment in order to reappear along strong and unmistakable lines. And this may never happen. We are thus faced with the possibility that childhood is a transitory aberration in cultural history, like the horse-drawn carriage or black scribbling on white paper.

To cheer myself up, I am willing to settle for the following formulation and hope that future research will confirm it: Childhood is analogous to language learning. It has a biological basis but cannot be realized unless a social environment triggers and nurtures it—that is, has need of it. If a culture is dominated by a medium that requires the segregation of the young in order that they learn specialized, complex skills and attitudes, then childhood, in one form or another, will emerge, articulate and indispensable. If the communication needs of a culture do not require the long-term segregation of the young, then childhood remains mute.

Let us proceed as if childhood is reclaimable, in some form. How can we give it a voice? There are three institutions that have a serious interest in the question: the family, the school, and government.

As for the first, it is as obvious as it is depressing that the structure and authority of the family have been severely weakened as parents have lost control over the information environment of the young. Margaret Mead once referred to television, for example, as the second parent, by which she meant that our children literally spend more time with television than with their fathers. In such terms, fathers may be the fifth or sixth parent, trailing behind television, the Internet, CDs, radio, and movies. Indeed, encouraged by the trend toward the devaluation of parenthood, Bell Telephone once had the effrontery to urge fathers to use "Dial-a-Story" as a substitute for telling their own stories to children. In any case, it is quite clear that the media have diminished the role of the family in shaping the values and sensibilities of the young.

Moreover, and possibly as a result of the enlarged sovereignty of the media, many parents have lost confidence in their ability to raise children because they believe that the information and instincts they have about child rearing are unreliable. As a consequence, they not only do not resist media influence, they turn to experts who are presumed to know what is best for children. Thus, psychologists, social workers, guidance counselors, teachers, and others representing an institutional point of view invade large areas of parental authority, mostly by invitation. What this means is that there is a loss in the intimacy, dependence, and loyalty that traditionally characterize the parent-child relationship. Indeed, it is now believed by some that the parent-child relationship is essentially neurotic, and that children are better served by institutions than by their families.

An effective response to all of this poses difficulties and is not without a price to pay. If parents wish to preserve childhood for their own children, they must conceive of parenting as an act of rebellion against culture. This is especially the case in America. For example, for parents merely to remain married is itself an act of disobedience and an insult to the spirit of a throwaway culture in which continuity has little value. It is also almost un-American to remain in close proximity to one's extended family so that children can experience, daily, the meaning of kinship and the value of deference and responsibility to elders. Similarly, to insist that one's children learn the discipline of delayed gratification, or modesty in their sexuality, or self-restraint in manners, language, and style is to place oneself in opposition to almost every social trend. But most rebellious of all is the attempt to control the media's access to one's children. There are, in fact, two ways to do this. The first is to limit the amount of exposure children have to media. The second is to monitor carefully what they *are* exposed to, and to provide them with a continuously running critique of the themes and values of the media's content. Both are very difficult to do and require a level of attention that most parents are not prepared to give to child-rearing.

Nonetheless, there are parents who are committed to doing all of these things, who are in effect defying the directives of their culture. Such parents are not only helping their children to *have* a childhood but are, at the same time, creating a sort of intellectual elite. Certainly in the short run, the children who grow up in such homes will, as adults, be much favored by business, the professions, and the media themselves. What can we say of the long run? Only this: Those parents who resist the spirit of the age will contribute to what might be called the Monastery Effect, for they will help to keep alive a humane tradition. It is not conceivable that our culture will forget that it has children. But it is halfway toward forgetting that children need childhood. Those who insist on remembering shall perform a noble service for themselves and their children.

There are two more points that need to be added about the family's role. In making them, I am aware that I will be misunderstood, but I am not such a coward as to let them pass. The first concerns the liberation of women from limited social roles, which I believe to be one of the truly humane ideas of the twentieth century. Nonetheless, nothing comes free. As women find their place in business, in the arts, and in the professions, there must be (almost by definition) a serious decline in the strength and meaning of traditional patterns of child care. For whatever criticisms may be made of the exclusive role of women as nurturers, the fact is that it is women, and women alone, who have been the overseers of childhood, shaping it and protecting it. It is unlikely that men will assume anything like the role women have played, and still do, in raising children, no matter how sensible it might be for men to do so. Thus, as parents of both sexes make their way in the world, children become something of a burden, and, increasingly, it is deemed best that their childhood end as early as possible. I know of nothing that can be done about this.

The second point is merely to observe that, in America, the fundamentalist movement (once called the Moral Majority) has been more aware of the decline of childhood than any other group in the body politic. Its attempts to organize economic boycotts against sponsors of certain television programs, its attempts to restore a sense of inhibition and reverence to sexuality, its attempts at setting up schools that insist on rigorous standards of civility, are examples of an active program aimed at preserving childhood. The liberal tradition (or, as fundamentalists contemptuously call it, secular humanism) has had pitifully little to offer in this matter. For example, in opposing economic boycotts of TV sponsors, civil libertarians have taken the curious position that it is better to have Procter & Gamble's moral standards control television content than Queen Victoria's. In any case, to the extent that a political philosophy can influence cultural change, the liberal tradition has tended to encourage the decline of childhood by its generous acceptance of all that is modern, and a corresponding hostility to anything that tries to "turn back the clock." But in some respects the clock is wrong, and fundamentalism may serve as a reminder of a world that was once hospitable to children and felt deeply responsible for what they might become. It is permissible, I think, for those of us who disapprove of the arrogance of fundamentalism to borrow some of their memories.

As for school, it is the only public institution left to us based on the assumption that there are important differences between childhood and adulthood. But the declining authority of school has been well documented, and, even worse, there is a widespread acceptance, as mentioned, of school as having only one purpose—to prepare the young for adult work. The question of how to nourish the souls of students—through art, for example— or how to cultivate taste (so that, to quote Karl Kraus, they might know the difference between an urn and a chamber pot) or how to promote a sense of educated patriotism (so that there is a continuing interest in knowing how their country was formed, and why) or how to think scientifically (so that it is understood that scientific thinking is not confined to scientists and has little to do with technology)—these and other concerns are moved to the rear and certainly not regarded as of importance to the education of consumers and job-seekers. Of course, there are exceptions to this trend, especially in those private schools that cling to some pre-twentieth-century theory—for example, the Rudolph Steiner schools and the Maria Montessori schools. For most of the rest, there is no operative influence of a humane educational theory—no Locke, no Rousseau, and for that matter, no Freud or Dewey.

But we may keep this in mind: The modern school was a creation of the printing press with movable type, for it was to school that the young were taken to learn how to be literate, and therefore how to be an adult. Is it possible that the computer may have a comparable effect? Not, I think, if all we wish to do is teach the young how to use computers, especially if we do so to help them in their "careers." That is easy to do and unnecessary, since most young people will learn how to use computers without help from schools. But suppose we wished them to learn how computers are programmed, how different computer languages do different things, how computers impose a particular world-view, how computers alter our definition of judgment, how computers change our conception of information and knowledge—then, indeed, the young will need school learning. But such a development would depend on many factors. It is not inevitable that the computer will be used to promote sequential, logical, complex, and even philosophical thought among the mass of people. There are economic and political interests that would be better served by allowing the bulk of a semiliterate population to entertain itself with the magic of visual computer games, to use and be used by computers without understanding. In this way the computer would remain mysterious and under the control of a bureaucratic elite. However, were our schools to grasp that a computer is not a tool but a philosophy of knowledge, we would

132

indeed have something to teach. And if we added to this a concern for art, science, literature, and all the rest schools once were thought to be interested in, the word "socialization" might have its meaning restored.

As I have mentioned, beginning in the eighteenth century, government came to play a role in maintaining the idea of childhood. Prohibiting the exploitation of child labor, treating children's crimes differently from the crimes of adults, imposing severe penalties for child abuse, and, of course, establishing public schools are examples of how, through legislation, government has assigned a special status to childhood. Most of these constraints and institutions are still in place, although in some cases they are weakening. For example, in America the differences between adults' and children's crimes are increasingly perceived as insignificant, and some states have adjusted their sentencing patterns to reflect an indifference to the age of a felon. There are also, to take another example, doubts raised about the mandatory nature of school attendance, and it would be no surprise if the maximum age for required school attendance were lowered. I might add, in this context, that we may expect the voting age to be lowered as well. The age of twenty-one was established at a time when literacy was assumed to be the key factor in one's ability to make a political choice, and it was assumed further that such an ability required time to mature. (As Tocqueville remarked early in the nineteenth century, "The politics of America is the politics of the printed word.") But with the emergence of nonprint forms of public communications, such as radio, film, and television, these assumptions became suspect, and the age was reduced to eighteen. I expect that within the lifetime of many of those reading this sentence, the age will be further reduced, perhaps to sixteen or even lower. After all, what are the arguments against it? That a sixteen-year-old does not have sufficient access to political information? That a sixteen-year-old has not yet developed sophisticated reading habits? That a sixteen-year-old does not yet know enough? How can he or she be effectively distinguished from the thirty-year-old who gets information from precisely the same sources?

Nonetheless, in spite of its diminishing importance, the idea of childhood—indeed, the word itself—still retains considerable emotional (perhaps nostalgic) power, and political figures commonly put themselves forward as its defenders. Many of them have correctly judged that the survival of the idea is connected in some way to the effects of media. As a consequence, legislation has been proposed to protect the young from violence and sexually explicit material on television and the Internet. From time to time, efforts are made to restrict certain kinds of advertising aimed at youth, and there is even legislation requiring that more time be given on television to "children's programming." (We should keep in mind that the movie rating system originated because of the fear of government legislation concerning the content of films.) Such proposals, and more of them, are to be encouraged, I think, although one ought not to expect them to have an enduring effect. For one thing, attempts to protect the young from the media continuously clash with the First Amendment to the Constitution, and civil libertarians fear the erosion of speech more than they fear the erosion of childhood. For another, the media are inextricably connected to commercial interests, and it is a rare politician who will stand clearly in opposition to such interests. I would offer here, as an example, Bill Clinton and Al Gore, both of whom were honorably active in promoting a mechanism (the V-chip) which allows parents to control television violence by blocking out certain programs. But neither one has had anything to propose or even to say about the crushing influence of television commercials. Since the federal government licenses broadcasters, and licensees are required to broadcast in the "public interest, convenience, and necessity," is it unthinkable to propose that commercials aimed at young children be forbidden? Well, yes, if your ambition is to achieve high political office, which cannot be realized without the support of corporate money. On the other hand, perhaps not. Although cigarette and hard liquor commercials are absent from television and radio only by industry policy, not by government decree, it is possible that a caring electorate might yet require the media industry to let our children go.

You may have the impression that I do not believe there is a realistic chance of childhood's surviving through the next century. Unless there is a serious and sustained public discussion about the matter (let us say, as much discussion as there was about Clinton's sexual appetite), I do not think there is. Electricity makes nonsense of the kind of information environment that gives rise to and nurtures childhood. We shall be fighting a losing battle here, sad to say. But in losing childhood, we would not have to lose everything. After all, the printing press shattered the cohesion of a world religious community, destroyed the intimacy and poetry of the oral tradition, diminished regional loyalties, and created a cruelly impersonal industrial system. And yet, Western civilization survived with some of its humane values intact and was able to forge new ones, including those associated with the nurturing of children. There is some ironic comfort in our remembering that we are still suffering from the shock of twentieth-century technology, which has numbed our brains so that it is difficult for us to notice some of the spiritual and social debris that our technology has strewn about us. We can expect the shock to wear off as we get to the other side of the bridge. When and if that happens, we may yet think of ways to preserve at least some form of childhood.

Chapter Eight

Democracy

In order to avoid an error some political scientists make, I am bound to begin this chapter by noting the obvious: Democracy is not a thing, a process, or an idea. It is a word, and a word that has had a checkered career at that. Its origin can be traced to the Greek city-states, and in its rough-and-tumble road it has been used to mean a multitude of things, not all of them pleasant. Plato, of course, would have none of it, since it implied giving power to those who had neither the intellectual resources nor the moral rigor to govern wisely. If he needed empirical proof of his political philosophy—which he didn't—he could find it in the judgment rendered against Socrates (by a vote of 280 to 220) which condemned the wisest man of Athens to death.

Aristotle was hardly less contemptuous of "democracy." He posited three kinds of government that are good and three that are bad. The good include monarchy, aristocracy, and constitutional government; the bad are tyranny, oligarchy, and democracy. Although he did not believe in equality any more than Plato, Aristotle introduced the curious qualification that when the worst—democracy—is corrupt, it is better than the best when the *best* is corrupt. Of course, what the Greeks meant by "democracy" was quite different from meanings more common today. Aristotle, for example, tells us that to elect magistrates is oligarchic, while to choose them by lot is democratic. We also know that the "demos"—the citizens of Athens who were eligible to participate in public affairs—consisted mostly of an elite class, excluding women, slaves, farmers, and, in general, those who earned their bread by the sweat of their brows. Of the 350,000 souls who lived in or close to Athens, only 20,000 qualified as citizens.

The Romans did not much favor "democracy," especially its implications of direct participation by "the people." They used the term "republic" to describe their system of consuls elected by a senate which was not indifferent to "vox populi." The word "democracy" barely stayed alive in Western civilization throughout the medieval period and the Renaissance but was retrieved with considerable energy in the seventeenth century, when political philosophy reawakened and the question of the nature and foundations of the state, and of political authority, assumed renewed importance.

With the exception perhaps of Machiavelli, Thomas Hobbes, no friend of "democracy," may be regarded as the first modern political theorist. His *Leviathan*, published in 1651, was exceedingly influential, largely as a justification of absolute monarchy. For Hobbes, the fundamental concern in governance was the maintenance of public order and so the avoidance of the mortal danger of anarchy. He was against the sharing of power and was not excessively troubled by despotism. Democracy in any form, he believed, would inevitably lead to anarchy. Hobbes's most influential opponent was John Locke, who, in 1689 and 1690, wrote his *Two Treatises on Government*. The first is a condemnation of the idea of hereditary power. In the second he put forward an idea that has attached itself to the word "democracy" to this day, even when the word is used by those who detest its referent. "The beginning of politic society," he wrote, "depends upon the consent of the individuals to join into and make one society." He introduced the idea of a "contract," borrowed, of course, although set in a different context, from the biblical covenant of the Jews with God. Rousseau used the same term later in his famous work *The Social Contract*, published in 1762. (It must be noted that Rousseau's argument for a social contract comes closer to Hobbes than to Locke, since Rousseau emphasized the obligation of the state to protect the individual; that is, protection from anarchy.)

Throughout the Enlightenment, the question of the source of legitimate authority and power was thoroughly explored, although Locke's idea of what might be called a "democratic polity" was not exactly what we have in mind today. Voltaire favored an "enlightened monarchy." Diderot wanted a "constitutional monarchy" (and tried to convert Catherine the Great to that view). Both Locke and Montesquieu favored a division of powers, but Rousseau clearly did not. Locke emphasized the importance of private property in any contract an individual makes with society. But not all Enlightenment philosophes, and not Rousseau in particular, were impressed with that idea.

As you can infer from these highly selective, fragmentary examples, I am not interested here in providing a history of the word "democracy." I am interested in making the point that any sentence that begins with "Democracy is . . . ," as if there is some essential, God-given meaning to the word, misleads us. Its meanings have varied widely, and its use in an unqualified positive sense is fairly recent. Indeed, as the word moved from Europe to America, it was certainly not greeted with the respect it is given today. American philosophes were mostly of a mixed mind as to what the word suggested. The word does not appear in the Declaration of Independence or the federal Constitution. Jefferson did call his party the Democrat-Republican to distinguish it from the Federalists. But in his first inaugural address, he said, "We are all Republicans, we are all Federalists"; he did not say, "We are all democrats." Many of America's founders—Alexander Hamilton and John Adams, for example—used the word in a pejorative sense. Adams considered democracy an ignoble and unjust form of government but was opposed to aristocracy largely on the grounds that aristocrats, being superior, were dangerous. We must keep in mind that the Founders (Gore Vidal refers to them as the Inventors) were men of wide learning and refined intellect, and were not without what we would call "elitist" tendencies. Jefferson was, on one occasion, denounced by Patrick Henry for "abjuring his native victuals"; that is to say, Jefferson liked French cooking. It should also be remembered that in America's beginnings, citizens did not directly vote for the president, vice-president, or members of the Senate; and, as noted earlier, the Founders favored a Roman conception of republicanism more than the Greek "democracy." The word's recent positive meanings have not always protected it from being used in ways that Plato, Aristotle, Hobbes, Locke, and all the rest would call despotism. In the 1930s, for example, the world's greatest dictators—Benito Mussolini, Adolf Hitler, and Joseph Stalin—used the word to praise the tyrannies they headed. In a speech in Berlin in 1937, Mussolini proclaimed that "the greatest and soundest democracies which exist in the world today are Italy and Germany." Stalin claimed that the Soviet Union was the most democratic regime in all history. And, of course, even today despots use the word to describe their regimes—indeed, are almost compelled to use it.

As we approach a new century, we can say that for most of us, the word has taken on a more or less settled meaning, and one that is wholly favorable. Its key part is the implication of the freely given consent of the governed to abide by the laws and policies of those agencies whose activities control the life of a community. Exactly how that consent is given expression and by whom and when is usually defined by some sort of constitution, which is subject to amendment. And to insure that those who have given their consent have done so without duress and as mature and thoughtful citizens, freedom of thought and speech must be allowed the widest possible latitude. When we add to this Kant's idea that persons are to be respected as an absolute end in themselves, and must not be used as a mere means for some external purpose, we have a fair description of what the word is presently taken to mean. In this description, I am saying nothing that any reader will find new or, I should think, disputable. What is missing from it is a point that is desperately important to those living now, and which Enlightenment thinkers addressed, even as they gifted us with the modern ideas we include under the heading of "democracy." The point can, in fact, be found as far back as Aristotle in his contention that democracy is best for small city-states, oligarchy for medium-sized states, and monarchy for large states; that is to say, that there is a relationship between the kind of government that is desirable and the means of communication that are available. Aristotle thought that, ideally, democracy implied that a person standing in the center of a city could, when giving an oration, be heard by all the citizens. Considering the fact that there were no amplification devices, one might think this unrealistic. However, Benjamin Franklin actually tested the idea (although for different reasons) in trying to determine exactly how far and by how many people the voice of the great orator Reverend Whitefield could be heard. His conclusion: from Market Street to a particular part of Front Street in Philadelphia, and by 30,000 people.

Putting Franklin's experiment aside, we may say that Enlightenment philosophes were not unaware of the connections between political life and communication. Indeed, Montesquieu gave considerable attention to the question of how an environment controls the forms of social life including the laws, the economy, and what he called the national character. In his *On the Spirit of Laws*, he is mostly concerned with the physical environment rather than the symbolic environment—that is to say, the natural ecology rather then the media ecology. He argued that the terrain—mountains or plateaus, jungles or desert, inland or coastal—is the basic determinant of social life. That there is some truth in this cannot be denied. But there may be greater truth in the idea that the means by which people communicate with each other, including their government, are the keys to how workable any system is. John Stuart Mill dwelt on this point, arguing that the active participation of the governed in the processes of government is an essential component of a democratic system. "The food of feeling," he wrote, "is action. . . . [L]et a person have nothing to do for his country, and he will not care for it." That, I assume, is what John F. Kennedy meant in saying, "Ask not what your country can do for you but what you can do for your country." Political indifference is the death of democracy. This is a point well understood by Tocqueville, who stressed the role played by political associations in giving health and vitality to the American system. He wrote:

> The inhabitant of the United States learns from birth that he must rely on himself to combat the ills and trials of life; he is restless and defiant in his outlook toward the authority of society and appeals to its power only when he cannot do without it. . . . If some obstacle blocks the public road halting the circulation of traffic, the neighbors at once form a deliberative body; this improvised assembly pro-

duces an executive authority which remedies the trouble
before anyone has thought of the possibility of some previously constituted authority beyond those concerned.[1]

Tocqueville, more than any other student of democracy, also
focused his attention on the role of media in giving American
form to democracy. By media (a word he did not, of course, use)
he meant the printed word. He wrote about the style of literary
expression in a democracy, and, in particular, how a democratic
polity produces a different literature than does an aristocracy.

Here, then, is a motley multitude with intellectual wants
to be supplied. These new votaries of the pleasure of the
mind have not all had the same education; they are not
guided by the same lights, do not resemble their own
fathers; and they themselves are changing every moment
with changing place of residence, feelings, and fortune. So
there are no traditions, or common habits, to forge links
between their minds, and they have neither the power nor
the wish nor the time to come to a common understanding. But it is from this heterogeneous, stirring crowd that
authors spring, and from it they must win profit and
renown.[2]

The only thing odd about this quotation is that it appears to
be a description when it is, in fact, a prophecy. For at the time it
was written American literature had not yet broken free of its
English roots, which Tocqueville regarded as reflecting an aristocratic tradition. One might say (as did Hemingway) that American literature begins with Mark Twain. Or, as I would prefer,
Edgar Allan Poe. In any case, early American literature is distinguished more by pamphlets and newspapers than by books. In

1786, Benjamin Franklin observed that Americans were so busy reading newspapers and pamphlets that they scarcely had time for books. (One book they apparently always had time for was Noah Webster's *American Spelling Book,* for it sold more than twenty-four million copies between 1783 and 1834.) Franklin's reference to pamphlets ought not to go unnoticed. The proliferation of newspapers in all the Colonies was accompanied by the rapid diffusion of pamphlets and broadsides. Tocqueville took note of this fact. "In America," he wrote, "parties do not write books to combat each other's opinions, but pamphlets, which are circulated for a day with incredible rapidity and then expire."[3] And he referred to both newspapers and pamphlets when he observed, "The invention of firearms equalized the vassal and the noble on the field of battle; the art of printing opened the same resources to the minds of all classes; the post brought knowledge alike to the door of the cottage and to the gate of the palace."[4] At the time Tocqueville was making his observations of America, printing had already spread to all the regions of the country. The South had lagged behind the North not only in the formation of schools but in its uses of the printing press. Virginia, for example, did not get its first regularly published newspaper, the *Virginia Gazette,* until 1736. But toward the end of the eighteenth century, the movement of ideas via the printed word was relatively rapid, and something approximating a national conversation emerged. For example, the *Federalist Papers,* an outpouring of eighty-five essays in defense of the proposed new Constitution, written by Alexander Hamilton, James Madison, and John Jay (all under the name of Publius), originally appeared in a New York newspaper during 1787 and 1788 but were read almost as widely in the South as in the North.

The influence of the printed word in every arena of public discourse was insistent and powerful not merely because of the quality of printed matter but because of its *monopoly*. This point cannot be stressed enough, especially for those who are reluctant to acknowledge profound differences in the media environments of then and now. One sometimes hears it said, for example, that there is more printed matter available today than ever before, which is undoubtedly true. But from the seventeenth century to the late nineteenth century, printed matter was virtually *all* that was available. There were no movies to see, radio to hear, photographic displays to look at, CDs to play. There was no television or Internet. Public business was channeled into and expressed through print, which became the model, the metaphor, and the measure of all discourse. The resonances of the linear, analytical structure of print, and in particular, of expository prose, could be felt everywhere—for example, in how people talked. Tocqueville remarks on this in *Democracy in America*. "An American," he wrote, "cannot converse, but he can discuss, and his talk falls into a dissertation. He speaks to you as if he were addressing a meeting; and if he should chance to become warm in the discussion, he will say 'Gentlemen' to the person with whom he is conversing."[5] This odd practice is less a reflection of an American's obstinacy than of his modeling his conversational style on the structure of the printed word. Since the printed word is impersonal and is addressed to an invisible audience, what Tocqueville is describing here is a kind of printed orality, which was observable in diverse forms of oral discourse. On the pulpit, for example, sermons were usually written speeches, delivered in a stately, impersonal tone, consisting, as Tocqueville remarked, "largely of an impassioned, coldly analytical cataloguing of the attributes of the Deity as revealed to man through Nature and Nature's Laws."

What I am driving at is that the modern conception of democracy was tied inseparably to the printed word. All the

Enlightenment political philosophers—none more explicitly than Locke, Madison, and Jefferson—assumed that political life would be conducted through print. We cannot hold it against them that they did not anticipate what we call the communications revolution. But we may borrow their minds to help us frame some questions about our present situation and in particular the future of what we call democracy.

The first question, then, might be: To what extent does a democratic polity depend upon the printed word? As we begin to answer such a question, Jefferson offers some encouragement about the process of change. "I know that laws and institutions," he said, "must go hand in hand with the progress of the human mind. As new discoveries are made, new truths disclosed, and manners and opinions change with the change of circumstances, institutions must change also and keep pace with the times."[6] This is indeed an encouragement to avoid being fearful of communication changes. But we, in turn, may ask of Jefferson: What changes, resulting from new discoveries and new technology, may be so vast that we will no longer be able to sustain a self-governing polity? Jefferson, I feel confident, would have at least two answers. The first is that as long as the rule of law would impel every person to oppose violations of public order, we are safe; and second, as long as there is a common understanding of inalienable rights, we cannot go wrong. ("Nothing is unchangeable," he wrote, "but the inherent and unalienable rights of man."[7]) And suppose we reply that the law, after all, was codified in and structured by the printed word, and that our conception of inalienable rights was equally expressed in writing. Do we not therefore depend upon respect for what is written? Do all the new media of this and future centuries enhance the power of the rule of law and help to convey and promote a unifying narrative? Jefferson, of course, has no answer to this question. And neither

145

do we—except for Lawrence Grossman, sort of. I have previously referred to his book *The Electronic Republic*. In it, he argues that the new interactive media will create the possibility of participatory democracy (as the Athenians practiced it) and will make representative democracy, as we now have it, obsolete. It will be possible for plebiscites to be held on every important question, so that citizens may decide directly and quickly on what policies their government shall pursue. In such a case, the printed word would be of diminished importance. Visual and aural media, along with print, will provide citizens with an abundance of information so that they will be qualified to make intelligent judgments. Jefferson's faith in the "people" would surely be tested by such "progress." Although he spoke of all people having equal rights, he assumed a minimum degree of intellectual competence—for example, literacy, not to mention historical knowledge and virtue—on the part of those who would directly participate in political affairs. Jefferson, in other words, would not be as impressed by the availability of information as he was by one's competence to understand and give coherent expression to political and social ideas. James Madison, the "father" of America's Constitution, would almost certainly disapprove of any tendencies toward direct democracy. "In a single republic," he wrote, "all the power surrendered by the people is submitted to the administration of a single government; and the usurpations are guarded against by a division of the government into distinct and separate departments."[8] Madison, in other words, would be worried about the usurpations of majority opinion, especially opinions that run counter to the Constitution.

We have, then, a question about the relationship between fast, visual, digital means of communication and the viability of "democracy," as we have come to understand it. As we walk across the metaphorical bridge to the new century, it would be worthwhile for citizens to discuss it—for *anybody* to discuss it. Do new media create a "plebiscite democracy"? And if they do, is this the direction we wish to go? Do the new media help to create what Alexander Hamilton might call "mobocracy"? Would Voltaire, Diderot, and Montesquieu find this a chilling prospect? Would Hobbes say, "This way leads only to anarchy; I warned you about this"?

I trust that it is not necessary for me to stress the point that we are under no obligation to follow the suggestions of Enlightenment philosophes. They knew nothing about instantaneous information, interactive media, merciless advertising messages, television political campaigns, and all the rest comprising "postmodern" culture. But since they invented our idea of "democracy," we would be wise to recall the assumptions on which they proceeded, none more urgent than the following: Democracy depends on public discourse, and therefore the kind and quality of the discourse is of singular importance. Simply to say that more information is received more quickly in diverse forms, with opportunities for fast feedback, is not to say that democratic processes are enriched. Grossman envisions a plebiscite or referendum democracy as a return to Athenian roots. But can five thousand educated, homogeneous Athenian men provide a model for two hundred fifty million multicultural, television-oriented citizens? Is giving an oration in the center of Athens or, for that matter, Philadelphia, the same thing as addressing citizens on television? Are we mocking democracy in creating an "electronic town hall meeting"? Does the Internet, as Tocqueville said of printing, open the same resources to the minds of all classes, and bring knowledge alike to the door of the cottage and to the gate of the palace? One way to locate where we are and where we might go in these matters is to focus on three characteristics of the eighteenth-century conception of democracy: language, individuality, and narrative. What follows, of course, is not the answers but the questions.

As for language, the philosophes might remind us that the written word and an oratory based upon it *have a content*—a semantic, paraphrasable content. Whenever language is the principal medium of communication—especially language controlled by the rigors of print—an idea, a fact, a claim is the inevitable result. The idea may be banal, the fact irrelevant, the claim false, but there is no escape from meaning when language is the instrument guiding one's thought. Though one may accomplish it from time to time, it is very hard to say nothing when employing a written sentence. What else is exposition good for? Words have very little to recommend them except as carriers of meaning. The shapes of written words are not especially interesting to look at. Even the sounds of sentences of spoken words are rarely engaging except when composed by those with extraordinary poetic gifts. If a sentence refuses to issue forth a fact, a request, a question, an assertion, an explanation, it is nonsense, a mere grammatical shell. As a consequence, a language-centered discourse such as was characteristic of eighteenth- and nineteenth-century America tends to be both content-laden and serious, all the more so when it takes its form from print.

It is serious because meaning demands to be understood. A printed sentence calls upon its author to say something, upon its reader to know the import of what is said. And when an author and reader are struggling with semantic meaning, they are engaged in the most serious challenge to the intellect. This is especially the case with the act of reading, for authors are not always trustworthy. They lie, they become confused, they overgeneralize, they abuse logic and, sometimes, common sense. The reader must come armed, in a serious state of intellectual readiness. This is not easy because the reader comes to the text alone.

In reading, one's responses are isolated, one's intellect thrown back on its own resources. To be confronted by the cold abstractions of printed sentences is to look upon language bare, without the assistance of either beauty or community. Thus, reading is by its nature a serious business. It is also, of course, an essentially rational activity.

From Erasmus in the sixteenth century to Elizabeth Eisenstein in the twentieth, almost every scholar who has grappled with the question of what reading does to one's habits of mind has concluded that the process encourages rationality; that the sequential, propositional character of the printed word fosters what Walter Ong calls the "analytic management of knowledge." To engage the written word means to follow a line of thought, which requires considerable powers of classifying, inference-making, and reasoning. It means to uncover lies, confusions, and overgeneralizations, to detect abuses of logic and common sense. It also means to weigh ideas, to compare and contrast assertions, to connect one generalization to another. To accomplish this, one must achieve a certain distance from the words themselves, which is, in fact, encouraged by the isolated and impersonal text. That is why a good reader does not cheer an apt sentence or pause to applaud even an inspired paragraph. Analytic thought is too busy for that, and too detached.

I do not mean to imply that prior to the written word, analytic thought was not possible. I am referring here not to the potentialities of the individual mind but to the predispositions of a cultural mind-set. In a culture dominated by print, public discourse tends to be characterized by a coherent, orderly arrangement of facts and ideas. The public for whom it is intended is generally competent to manage such discourse. In a print culture, writers make mistakes when they lie, contradict themselves, fail to support their generalizations, try to enforce illogical connections. In a print culture, readers make mistakes when they don't notice, or even worse, don't care.

In the eighteenth and nineteenth centuries, print put forward a definition of intelligence that gave priority to the objective, rational use of the mind and at the same time encouraged forms of public discourse with serious, logically ordered content. It is no accident that the Age of Reason was coexistent with the growth of a print culture, first in Europe and then in America.

We must come back, then, to the first question and ask ourselves, not Jefferson, Does any decline in the significance of the printed word make democracy less rational? Can a representative democracy, even a participatory democracy, function well if its citizens' minds are not disciplined by the printed word? Those who are the cheerleaders for digital processes are not concerned with this question. They look straight ahead with a giddy and aggressive optimism to a world of easy and fast access to information. And that is enough for them. The slower, linear, reflective forms characteristic of print are not taken by them to represent a philosophy of thought, a mind-set, a way of ordering knowledge. For the most part, they do not think that intelligence, rationality, and critical judgment have much to do with *forms* of communication. In this belief they may be colossally mistaken. Shall we remind them that the people who *invented* the digital age— indeed, invented the communications revolution—were themselves educated by the printed word? Does this tell us something important? Is there anything to be learned by recalling what the "guru of the Electronic Age," Marshall McLuhan, said about the book as it increasingly ceases to be, as he put it, the ordinary and pervasive environment? He remarked in a letter to a publisher that we must "approach the book as a cultural therapy, an indispensable ingredient in communal diet, necessary for the maintenance of civilized values as opposed to tribal values."[9] Is it possible that as print loses its dominance, the underpinnings of a democratic polity crumble? As we cross the bridge to the new century, shouldn't we at least chat about this? Or are we too enchanted by the information superhighway to notice that there might be a problem at the other end?

I would suggest that we also need to chat about another question: To what extent do the new media promote egoism, and therefore undermine the sense of community without which a democratic polity cannot function? I use the word "egoism" in the same sense as it was used by Tocqueville. In *Democracy in America*, he distinguishes between individualism and egoism. After noting that "individualism" was a recently coined word (he was writing in the 1840s), Tocqueville uses it to refer to "a calm and considered feeling which disposes each citizen to isolate himself from the mass of his fellows and withdraw into the circle of family and friends; with this little society formed to his taste, he gladly leaves the greater society to look after itself."[10] Tocqueville argues that individualism is of democratic origin but is too easily transformed into egoism, which "sterilizes the seeds of every virtue" and makes democracy impossible; that is, egoism is individualism writ large and ugly, so that feelings of and for community life are alien, if not incomprehensible. He suggests that individualism is a problem for democracy but that democracy can survive it. Egoism is another matter.

We know of the role played by the printing press with movable type in promoting individualism. It greatly amplified, for example, the quest for fame and individual achievement. "It is no accident," Elizabeth Eisenstein remarks in *The Printing Press as an Agent of Change*, "that printing is the first 'invention' which became entangled in a priority struggle and rival national claims."[11] Why no accident? Because, she suggests, the possibility of having one's words and work fixed forever created a new and pervasive idea of selfhood. The printing press is nothing less than a time-machine, easily as potent and as curious as any one of H. G. Wells's contraptions. Like the mechanical clock, which was also a great time-machine, the printing press captures, domesticates, and transforms time, and in the process alters humanity's consciousness of itself. But whereas the clock, as Lewis Mumford contends, eliminated eternity as the measure and focus of human actions, the printing press restored it. Printing links the present with forever. It carries personal identity into realms unknown. With the printing press, forever may be addressed by the voice of an individual, not a social aggregate.

What sort of time-machines are the newer media—television, computers, CDs, faxes? Even more important, what transformations in consciousness do they promote? Does anyone know? Is it a matter widely discussed? Most of the new media, like the printed word, are "private" in the sense that they do not require a community context. We see movies at home, frequently alone. We watch television in the same way, and listen to radio and music largely alone. We send and receive e-mail messages alone. It seems that now we even go bowling alone.[12] Of course, reading, as St. Jerome noted many centuries ago, is an antisocial activity. What do we require of others when we are reading? Their absence. If not that, their silence. That is why the printed word promoted individualism. ("The scribal culture," Eisenstein remarks, "held narcissism in check. Printing released it.") But if printed forms of communication increased our consciousness of selfhood, what happens when we have many media that are "privatizing"? Does this merge individualism into egoism? Are we gradually losing the sense of community wherein, as Tocqueville described it, Americans quickly and habitually join together to solve problems, and do so long before the central government is even aware of a problem? It is necessary to keep in mind here—

especially for those who believe e-mail and the Internet provide new opportunities for community—that we too easily confuse simulations with reality; that is to say, electronic community is only a simulation of community. A real, functional political community requires the nuance and directness of the human voice, face-to-face confrontations and negotiations with differing points of view, the possibilities of immediate action.

Which leads to a final consideration. I devoted an earlier chapter to narrative and have no intention of saying much more about it here. But in the context of the future of "democracy," it needs to be noted that our conception of the word's meaning is, itself, a myth, a kind of fantasy about what ought to be. But such fantasies, when shared by all, connect individuals to each other, providing a common language, a set of ideals, and a program for the future. The Declaration of Independence, the Constitution, the Gettysburg Address, Martin Luther King Jr.'s "I Have a Dream" speech are all fantasies, in the sense I am using the word. These fantasies, these dreams, are the legacy of the Enlightenment and have served as the foundation of how we define "democracy." The question, therefore, must arise, Do the new media of communication help or hinder in the development of shared dreams of democracy? Do our movies, TV shows, and songs bind us or loosen us?

There are, of course, other factors that can threaten the maintenance of a common political and national narrative—a "global economy" is one. But a discussion of that would require a whole book of its own. Here I raise the point that the fantasies and dreams of what we have come to call "democracy" were created by masters of the printed word. What new dreams will be created by masters of digital communication? And whose definition of "democracy" will it include? I have no ready or even nearly ready answers to these questions. It is better to disappoint one's readers than to mislead them. What I am asking for is a serious conversation about the relationship between our new media and our old democracy. Grossman, in *The Electronic Republic*, begins such a conversation. I have intended in this chapter to add to it. And I am hoping it will be continued—even if only on television.

Chapter Nine

Education

There are three clear legacies of the eighteenth century that bear on education; that is to say, on schooling. The first, an outgrowth of the "invention" of childhood itself, is the idea that schooling must be based on an understanding of the nature of childhood and, in particular, of the different stages through which the young travel on their journey to adulthood. The second, an outgrowth of the emergence of the nation-state, is the idea that an educated populace is a national resource. And the third is the assumption that an educated mind is practiced in the uses of reason, which inevitably leads to a skeptical—one might even say a scientific—outlook. Of the first two I will say little, since they are ideas about which there is no dispute. They are firmly rooted in education discourse and will be carried without challenge into the future. The third requires considerable discussion.

As to the first, we might say that its origin is to be found in Rousseau's *Emile*, published in 1762. I have previously referred to *Emile* but may not have stressed the extent to which it caused a sensation in its time and changed the nature of thought about education. Emile is an orphan whose education is guided for twenty-five years by a man of sensitivity and intellectual depth. Emile is removed from society, having only his tutor as a companion. The boy learns only what he feels a need to know, at his own pace. He does not learn to read or write until he is twelve, and then only because he feels a need to do so. His tutor does not "teach" in the usual sense of the word but tries to put Emile in situations from which he might see the need for learning. The learning, Emile does for himself. This, Rousseau believed, is the "natural" way education proceeds, and he assures us that those who are educated in this way will be well prepared for manhood in society (a society, incidentally, of which they would know next to nothing).

To this day, no one (not even A. S. Neill of Summerhill) has taken *Emile* literally, but much of what has passed for education in the West has been influenced by it, especially the idea that we ought to think about schooling from the point of view of those who are being schooled.

At the time *Emile* was published, there lived in Zurich a sixteen-year-old named Johann Heinrich Pestalozzi, of whom we might say that he became the first modern curriculum specialist. He grasped early that the ways in which schooling was conducted did not take children seriously. Unlike Rousseau, Pestalozzi actually liked children, and as he grew he increased his knowledge of and sensitivity to them. In a diary he kept early in his career, one can easily see the influence of Rousseau on Pestalozzi's views of education. "Let the child be as free as possible," he wrote, "treasure every moment which may be conducive to freedom, peace, and equanimity. Do not teach by words anything which you can teach by actual experience of things as they are."[1] He converted a farm into what he hoped would be a self-supporting industrial school, and, in 1765, opened its doors to twenty children, all of them from poor families. This school, and others with which Pestalozzi was associated, gave him a perspective Rousseau did not have: knowledge of actual children. Pestalozzi eventually developed principles for and methods of teaching everything from reading and writing to moral rectitude. Although he never abandoned the principle of self-activity, he departed sharply from Rousseau in that he offered courses of study, was deeply concerned with socializing children, and even allowed corporal punishment in special cases. His book *How Gertrude Teaches Her Children* (published in 1801) made him famous as an educator and in due course exerted influence on Friedrich Froebel. Froebel studied briefly with Pestalozzi and acknowledged the importance of the Pestalozzian principle of stressing concrete knowledge rather than abstract theory. But he judged Pestalozzi's approach to be superficial and one-sided, and in 1816 opened his own school, called somewhat pretentiously (he had only five students) the "Universal German Educational Institute." In 1840, Froebel gave us the name "kindergarten" for schools he founded in Blankenburg and Rudolfstadt.

I mention all this to give some weight to the claim that a "child-centered" education is a gift of the Enlightenment, and, one might add, a precious one. Although there is, from time to time, a movement toward a "subject-centered" education (for example, recently, in the approach of E. D. Hirsch or Alan Bloom, and, as you will see a few pages from now, me), no modern educator ignores the nature of the learner (well, perhaps Bloom). Teaching and learning are now understood as transactional, which is to say, we understand that there is no sense in saying you have taught something if it has not been learned. (Can you say that you have sold something to me even though I didn't buy it?) Perhaps teachers do not always act as if they believed that, but they know that it is the learner who matters, and that how learning is facilitated is the essential problem pedagogy must solve. We can fairly say that this orientation is a product of eighteenth-century thought. Since then we have not at any time abandoned that way of thinking and will carry it into the future.

As for the second gift of the Enlightenment—that education

is a national resource—it is an idea that emerged at roughly the same time as the first. In fact, the year after *Emile* appeared, De la Chalotais published an essay on national education. The essay was largely an attack on the Jesuits, who, at the time, controlled education in France. But it was more than that, since he argued persuasively for the value to a nation of an educated populace. The idea took hold—was, in fact, in the air—and led to movements toward making education a national affair throughout Europe. Even Frederick the Great, ruler of Prussia, gave up his belief that the greater the ignorance of the people, the easier it is to govern them. Under his leadership, education laws were passed in 1763 and 1765, making elementary education a state matter and requiring compulsory education for all children from five to thirteen years of age.

In its formative stages, education in America was connected almost wholly to religion. (It was essential, for example, for Protestants to be able to read the Bible.) But by the time Paine, Priestley, Jefferson, Adams, Madison, and Franklin were defining American democracy, the importance of education for political reasons was clear. Priestley formulated a philosophy of education that was to provide children with models of sound democratic thought, which included not only scientific knowledge but a scientific outlook. He was the first educator, perhaps in all history, to conduct laboratory experiments in a schoolroom. Jefferson, in his argument for universal public education, stressed the point that America needed to exploit all of its intellectual resources. Britain, France, and other European nations chose their national leaders from the uppermost tenth of the population. America, being smaller than those nations, could not afford to do so. "By that part of our plan which prescribes the selection of youths of genius from among the classes of the poor," Jefferson wrote, "we hope to avail the State of those talents which Nature has sown as liberally among the poor as among the rich, but which perish without use."[2] Franklin, of course, helped to found a college, and almost all of the Founders studied the history and literature of the ancient world (Plutarch, Thucydides, and Tacitus, among others) and held that a democratic citizenry needed to know the ways in which the Greeks and Romans governed themselves.

The idea that a nation-state of democratic aspirations requires an educated citizenry has been continuously advanced from the eighteenth century to the present day, and no political leader, then or now, did or will speak against it. One must acknowledge, of course, that in our own time, especially in America, the argument for education is largely based on a nation's economic needs. Typically, the argument is advanced that a nation will not be able to compete economically with other nations unless its youth has a proper education. What is a "proper education" is much debated, but the point is that education is conceived of as a national project, even in America, which features "local control" over the curriculum. Americans are much distressed when comparative testing reveals that the youth of Japan or Germany or Sweden (or wherever) score higher than do American youth. Why they should care is explained by the assumption that brainpower is considered to be among the more important resources of a nation. No one questions this assumption, and we will carry it with us to any futures we will confront.

We come then to the third legacy of the Enlightenment: the idea that a "proper education" must have as one of its goals the cultivation of a skeptical outlook based on reason. Although this idea is implicit in the writings of eighteenth-century educators, it comes to us mostly in the writings of eighteenth-century philosophes. Indeed, if the question is posed, What is the principal mind-set associated with the Enlightenment?, the answer would certainly be—skepticism. Modern educators do not usually use this word, preferring something like "critical thinking." But in any case, they do not do much about it.

There are several reasons why. The first is that it is dangerous. Were we to allow, indeed, encourage, our children to think critically, their questioning of constituted authority would almost certainly be one result. We might even say that "critical thinking" works to undermine the idea of education as a national resource, since a free-thinking populace might reject the goals of its nation-state and disturb the smooth functioning of its institutions.

Another reason is that it is by no means clear that parents want such an education for their children. Any educational project involves, in varying degrees, the risk of alienating children from their parents. And the idea that the young should be educated to be skeptical is dangerous not only to a nation-state but to the equanimity of the home.

There is at least one other reason why such an education is problematic: There is no guarantee that it works. By itself, that is no reason to avoid it, since there is no guarantee that *anything* done to or for children in school works. Nonetheless, the school curriculum is always a kind of wager that one sort of thing is more valuable to try than another, and there are those who hold that experiments in "critical thinking" are not worth the bet.

But let us suppose, as Jefferson did and, much later, John Dewey, that a democratic society must take the risk, that such a society will be improved by citizens of a critical mind, and that the best way for citizens to protect their liberty is for them to be encouraged to be skeptical, to be suspicious of authority, and to be prepared (and unafraid) to resist propaganda. And let us suppose further that at least some parents believe it to be an important goal and will raise no objections against it. We would then confront another major problem: How do you teach reason and

160

skepticism? Experience has shown that this is very difficult to do. Teachers are usually not trained to do it, and students are not accustomed to the rigor of it. One may even say that the very structure of school—its grading system, its course requirements, its tests—militates against it. Nonetheless, I shall complete this chapter with five suggestions as to how it might be done, and will end the book on that note. As I remarked earlier, skepticism is the principal legacy of the Enlightenment. There is nothing more profound to do than to carry that legacy forward by making an effort at conveying it to our young.

The first suggestion is not especially controversial but is nonetheless the least likely to be taken seriously. I refer to the possibility that we would actually teach children something about the art and science of asking questions. No one, I assume, would deny that all the knowledge we have is a result of our asking questions; indeed, that question-asking is the most significant intellectual tool human beings have. Is it not curious, then, that the most significant intellectual skill available to human beings is not taught in school? I can't resist repeating that: The most significant intellectual skill available to human beings is not taught in school. There may be those who can remember some teacher spending a day or two, or maybe even a week, on the subject of how to ask questions, of what kinds of different questions there are, of how different subjects are characterized by different questions, of the relationship between the questions we ask and the answers we get. But I doubt that there is anyone who can say that any of this was taught in a sustained and systematic way in school. And I doubt further that anyone knows of a school where this is done. When educators talk about developing "critical thinking" skills, they almost never include question-asking as one of them. For thirty-five years, I have tried to discover why question-asking is not considered a core subject in school. None of the answers I

Building a Bridge to the 18th Century

have considered seem adequate, among them, intellectual innocence among teachers, the failure of anyone to devise a test to
measure competence in this skill, the fact that teachers themselves did not study the subject in school, and the fact that school
is traditionally considered a place for students to learn answers,
not the questions which evoke the answers. It is possible that
teachers and school administrators know intuitively that serious
work in the art and science of question-asking is politically explo-
sive, and therefore give it a wide berth. What will happen if a student, studying history, asks, "Whose history is this?" What will
happen if a student, having been given a definition (of anything)
asks, "Who made up this definition? Are there other ways to
define this thing?" What will happen if a student, being given a
set of facts, asks, "What is a fact? How is it different from an
opinion? And who is the judge?" What happens, of course, is that
students not only learn "history," "definitions," and "facts"
(which Bloom and Hirsch want them to learn) but also learn
where these things come from and why (which Bloom and
Hirsch don't care about). Such learning is at the heart of reasoning and its product, skepticism. Do we dare do such a thing?
Have you heard anyone talk about this? The president, the secre-
tary of education, a school superintendent? They want our students to be answer-givers, not question-askers. They want
students to be believers, not skeptics. They want to measure the
quantity of answers, not the quality of questions (which, in any
case, is probably not measurable). Those who think otherwise,
who think an active, courageous, and skillful question-asker is
precisely what a "proper education" should produce, can take
comfort and inspiration from Voltaire, Hume, Franklin, Priestley, and Jefferson. Surely they would applaud the effort.

A second suggestion is related to the first in that it is also
about language. Twenty-three hundred years ago, educators

162

devised a pattern of instruction whose purpose was to help students defend themselves against both the seductions of eloquence and the appeal of nonsense. The pattern was formalized in the Middle Ages, and came to be known as The Trivium. It included logic, rhetoric, and grammar. This tradition survives among modern American educators in a truncated form: They teach the one subject among the three—grammar—that is the least potent, the least able to help students do what we call critical thinking. In fact, grammar, which takes up about a third of the English curriculum in junior high school, is not even taught with a view toward helping students think critically. Indeed, it is difficult to know why grammar, as it is presently taught, is included in the curriculum at all. Since the early 1900s, studies have been conducted to discover if there is any relationship between the teaching of grammar and a variety of language behaviors, such as reading and writing. Almost without exception, the studies have found no positive relationship whatsoever.

Although the other two subjects, logic and rhetoric, sometimes go by different names today—among them, practical reasoning, semantics, and general semantics—I would suggest, whatever we call them, that they be given a prominent place in the curriculum. These subjects are about the relationship between language and reality; they are about the differences among kinds of statements, about the nature of propaganda, about the ways in which we search for truths, and just about everything else one needs to know in order to use language in a disciplined way and to know when others aren't. With all the talk these days about how we are going through an information revolution, I should think that the question of what language skills are necessary to survive it would be uppermost in teachers' minds. I know that educational research is not always useful, and sometimes absurd, but for what it may be worth, a clear and positive

163

relationship between the study of semantics and critical thinking is well established in the research literature. As with the absence of question-asking from the curriculum, the absence of semantics—the study of the relationship between the world of words and the world of non-words—is also something of a mystery, if not an outrage.

Whatever else we bring into the new century, we will certainly feature the greatest array of propagandistic techniques in the history of humankind. I find it interesting to speculate on what Voltaire or Kant or Hume or Jefferson would advise on how to protect the young from the devastating effects of this assault. It is possible that one or two of them might conclude that reason cannot survive such a situation. But we cannot afford the luxury of so depressing a conclusion.

This is not the place to provide details as to how education can help the young defend themselves against propaganda in all its seductive varieties, but a serious attempt at language study is, I believe, the key. And, of course, it must begin with the idea that words are not only tools to think with but, for all practical purposes, the content of our thoughts. I am not implying that the world consists only of words; that is to say, I am not a modern French philosopher. I am saying that whatever meanings we give to the world—what sense we make of things—derive from our power to name, to create vocabularies. The process by which words and other symbols give shape and substance to our thoughts can be suggested by your trying to describe to another person what goes on in the place we call *school* but without using such terms as school, teacher, student, principal, test, grades, subject, course, curriculum, syllabus, homework, or any of the more or less technical terms which comprise the vocabulary of that semantic environment. I think it can be done—though, to be sure, with considerable difficulty—and my guess is that what you will end up describing will be barely recognizable as a "school." Perhaps it will sound like a prison or a hospital or a rehabilitation center. It depends. And it depends on what words you use in place of those you have given up.

Consider the two different vocabularies that are commonly used to describe the use of pharmaceuticals. One of them you will hear every fifteen minutes or so on television. "Mother!" shouts an irate young woman. "I can do it myself!" What's wrong with her? She is "upset," her "nerves are jangled," she's not "feeling well," she can't go on with her "work." The recommended solution is to take a drug—aspirin, Bufferin, tranquilizers, Nytol. The language here is the language of illness and medical care, and on that account, I assume, the narcotics agents pay it no attention. But what the audience is being advised to take can also be called "uppers" or "downers." We are being asked to "turn off and turn on," to get "high." These terms are, of course, part of the language of the streets. Well, which is it? Are we restoring equanimity to our troubled lives or are we "blowing our minds"? It depends, doesn't it, on what you call it, and why.

This is why in discussing what words we shall use in describing an event, we are not engaging in "mere semantics." We are engaged in trying to control the perceptions and responses of others (as well as ourselves) to the character of the event itself. And that is why people who understand this fact wince when someone gets ready to "tell it like it is." No one can tell anything "like it is." In the first place, it isn't anything until someone names it. In the second place, the way in which "it" is named reveals not the way it *is* but how the namer wishes to see it or is capable of seeing it. And third, how it has been named becomes the reality for the namer and all who accept the name. But it need not be *our* reality.

Take, for example, the type of man who is conventionally

called a "Roman Catholic priest." If you accept this name, you will not think him insane for deliberately abstaining from sexual intercourse for his entire lifetime. If you do not accept this name, you will think such a man is badly in need of psychiatric help. By "accepting" the name, I mean that you agree to its legitimacy, that you judge the semantic environment within which it occurs to be reasonable and purposeful. Above all, you accept the assumptions upon which it rests. Well, what shall we say, then, of a "priest"? How can we tell it like it really is? Is he displaying "psychotic symptoms" or is he displaying "his devotion to God"?

The point is well made in the story of the three umpires. The first umpire, being a man of small knowledge of how meanings are made, says, "I calls 'em as they are." The second umpire, knowing something about human perception and its limitations, says, "I calls 'em as I sees 'em." The third umpire, having been given some instruction in the role of language in human affairs, says, "Until I calls 'em, they ain't."

This does not mean, of course, that some umpires are not better than others. What you call something tells a great deal about how well and how widely you can see. After all, the umpire who calls "it" strike three, when everyone else sees the pitch sail over the batter's head, is usually called "blind." That is to say, we are not obliged to accept the labels other people supply. These ideas—that people create meanings by the names they use, and that we are free to reject the names that are given (whether in the realm of politics, commerce, or religion)—are central to language education, and are one's principal source of defense against a culture in which propaganda is the largest industry.

My third suggestion concerns the teaching of a scientific outlook. I mean by this phrase something different from what is usually meant by "science." The latter term suggests instruction in physics, biology, chemistry, and related disciplines. No one, I

Education

take it, will dispute the importance of teaching such subjects, but their inclusion in the curriculum does not insure that students will develop a scientific mind-set. The science curriculum is usually focused on communicating the known facts of each discipline without serious attention (i.e., without *any* attention) to the history of the discipline, the mistakes scientists have made, the methods they use and have used, or the ways in which scientific claims are either refuted or confirmed. Of course, a school that takes question-asking and semantics seriously is halfway toward conveying a sense of scientific thinking. But there is more to it than that, and as an example of what is at stake, I offer the argument between "evolution" and "creation science." Like evolution, creation science purports to explain how the world and all that's in it came to be, but it does so by taking the Bible as an infallible account of the world's history. More and more people believe in creation science, and not a few of them have taken the inevitable line that their belief is infused with sufficient respectability to be included in the school curriculum. In response to this, many scientists rush to defend evolution by seeking to banish creation science. In doing so, they sound much like those legislators who in 1925 prohibited by law the teaching of evolution in Tennessee. In that case, anti-evolutionists were fearful that a scientific idea would undermine religious belief. In the present case, pro-evolutionists are fearful that a religious idea will undermine scientific belief. The former had insufficient confidence in religion; the latter have insufficient confidence in science.

Good science has nothing to fear from bad science, and by our putting one next to the other, the education of our youth would be served exceedingly well. I would propose that evolution and creation science be presented in schools as alternative theories. Here is why:

167

Building a Bridge to the 18th Century

In the first place, Darwin's explanation of how evolution happened *is* a theory. So is the updated version of Darwin. Even the "fact" that evolution occurred is based on high levels of inference and supposition. Fossil remains, for example, are sometimes ambiguous in their meaning and have generated diverse interpretations. And there are peculiar gaps in the fossil record, which is something of an enigma, if not an embarrassment, to evolutionists.

The story told by creationists is also a theory. That a theory has its origins in a religious metaphor or belief is irrelevant. Not only was Newton a religious mystic but his conception of the universe as a kind of mechanical clock constructed and set in motion by God is about as religious an idea as you can find. What is relevant is the question, To what extent does a theory meet scientific criteria of validity? The dispute between evolutionists and creation scientists offers textbook writers and teachers a wonderful opportunity to provide students with insights into the philosophy and methods of science. After all, what students really need to know is not whether this or that theory is to be believed, but how scientists judge the merit of a theory. Suppose students were taught the criteria of scientific theory evaluation and then were asked to apply these criteria to the two theories in question. Wouldn't such a task qualify as authentic science education?

To take another example: Most useful theories invoke unseen forces to explain observable events. But the unseen forces (e.g., gravity) should be capable of generating fairly reliable predictions. Does the invocation of God in creation science meet this criterion? Does natural selection?

I suspect that when these two theories are put side by side, and students are given the freedom to judge their merit as science, creation theory will fail ignominiously (although natural selection is far from faultless). In any case, we must take our chances. It is not only bad science to allow disputes over theory to go unexamined, but also bad education.

Some argue that the schools have neither the time nor the obligation to take notice of every discarded or disreputable scientific theory. "If we carried your logic through," a science professor once said to me, "we would be teaching post-Copernican astronomy alongside Ptolemaic astronomy." Exactly. And for two good reasons. The first was succinctly expressed in an essay George Orwell wrote about George Bernard Shaw's remark that we are more gullible and superstitious today than people were in the Middle Ages. Shaw offered as an example of modern credulity the widespread belief that the Earth is round. The average man, Shaw said, cannot advance a single reason for believing this. (This, of course, was before we were able to take pictures of the Earth from space.) Orwell took Shaw's remark to heart and examined carefully his own reasons for believing the world to be round. He concluded that Shaw was right: that most of his scientific beliefs rested solely on the authority of scientists. In other words, most students have no idea why Copernicus is to be preferred over Ptolemy. If they know of Ptolemy at all, they know that he was "wrong" and Copernicus was "right," but only because their teacher or textbook says so. This way of believing is what scientists regard as dogmatic and authoritarian. It is the exact opposite of scientific belief. Real science education would ask students to consider with an open mind the Ptolemaic and Copernican world-views, array the arguments for and against each, and then explain why they think one is to be preferred over the other.

A second reason to support this approach is that science, like any other subject, is distorted if it is not taught from a historical perspective. Ptolemaic astronomy may be a refuted scientific theory but, for that very reason, it is useful in helping students to see that knowledge is a quest, not a commodity; that what we think we know comes out of what we once thought we knew; and that what we will know in the future may make hash of what we now believe.

Of course, this is not to say that every new or resurrected explanation for the ways of the world should be given serious attention in our schools. Teachers, as always, need to choose—in this case by asking which theories are most valuable in helping students to clarify the bases of their beliefs. Ptolemaic theory, it seems to me, is excellent for this purpose. And so is creation science. It makes claims on the minds and emotions of many people; its dominion has lasted for centuries and is thus of great historical interest; and in its modern incarnation, it makes an explicit claim to the status of science.

It remains for me to address the point (not quite an argument) that we dare not admit creation science as an alternative to evolution because most science teachers do not know much about the history and philosophy of science, and even less about the rules by which scientific theories are assessed; that is to say, they are not equipped to teach science as anything but dogma. If this is true, then we should take action at once to correct a serious deficiency, i.e., by improving the way science teachers are educated.

My fourth suggestion concerns what I call "technology education." As I have said and implied in the chapter on technology, I do *not* mean by technology education teaching our youth how to use computers. Forty-five million Americans have already figured out how to use computers without any help whatsoever from the schools. If the schools do nothing about this in the next ten years, everyone will know how to use computers. But what they will *not* know, as none of us did about everything from automobiles to movies to television, is what are the psychological, social, and political effects of new technologies. And that is a

170

subject that ought to be central in schools. It requires some knowledge of the history of technology, of the principles of technological change, and of the economic and social alterations that technology inevitably imposes. If we want our students to live intelligently in a technological society, I don't see how this can be done if they are ignorant of the full meaning and context of technological change. I should add here, based on my own observation of students in foreign lands, that on the question of the history and effects of technology, American students are the most ignorant group I have yet come across. The average American graduate student cannot tell you, given a thousand-year margin of error, when the alphabet was invented, or, given a two-hundred-year margin of error, when the printing press with movable type was invented, let alone say anything intelligible about the psychological or social implications of those inventions. To think that these are the people to whom we will entrust the uses of the information superhighway would be laughable if it weren't so dangerous.

Let me be clear on this point. I raise no objection to a school's wiring classrooms to the Internet or bringing personal computers to students, provided, of course, that the school has plenty of money; that is, pays its teachers well, can hire enough teachers to significantly reduce class size, and has no shortage of up-to-date books. My point is that, if we are going to make technology education part of the curriculum, its goal must be to teach students to use technology rather than to be used by it. And that means that they must know how a technology's use affects the society in which they live, as well as their own personal lives. This is something we did not do with television, and, I fear, we are not now doing with computer technology.

My fifth and final suggestion, easily the most controversial, concerns religion. I am aware, of course, that the words "religion" and "public schools" do not go together, at least not in America. They are like magnets that, upon getting too close, repel each other. There are good reasons for this, among them the First Amendment, which, even before it mentions freedom of speech, prohibits Congress from establishing a national religion. This has been wisely interpreted to mean that public institutions may not show any preference for one religion over another. It has also been taken to mean, not so wisely, that public institutions should show no interest in religion at all. One consequence of this is that public schools are barely able to refer to religion in almost any context. But I think ignoring religion is a serious mistake.

There are several reasons for this. One is that so much of our painting, music, architecture, literature, *and* science is intertwined with religion. It is, therefore, quite impossible (impossible by definition) for anyone to claim to be educated who has no knowledge of the role played by religion in the formation of culture. Another reason is that the great religions are, after all, the stories of how different people of different times and places have tried to achieve a sense of transcendence. Although many religious narratives provide answers to the questions of how and when we came to be, they are all largely concerned with answering the question, Why? Is it possible to be an educated person without having considered questions of why we are here and what is expected of us? And is it possible to consider these questions by ignoring the answers provided by religion? I think not, since religion may be defined as our attempt to give a total, integrated response to questions about the meaning of existence.

I therefore propose that, beginning sometime in late elementary school and proceeding with focused detail in high school and beyond, we provide our young with opportunities to study comparative religion. Such studies would promote no particular religion but would aim at illuminating the metaphors, literature, art, and ritual of religious expression itself.

Were we to make the subject of comparative religion part of the education of our youth, there would arise many questions and difficulties to which I have no answers, and, I feel sure, other teachers have no answers either. But our ignorance does not rule the subject out. To do it, we would have to proceed with mature preparation. This implies that there need to be national, regional, and local teacher conferences and institutes devoted to the ways in which comparative religion might be taught, so that teachers can learn from one another what the difficulties might be and how to overcome them. Does this seem too much to ask? Why is it that nothing is easier to organize, is better funded, and is better attended than a conference on how to teach computers? Is it certain that teacher interest can be aroused only about technical or technological matters? Are we too stupid or fearful to discuss the opportunities offered by religious diversity? I hope not.

I suspect readers have noticed that my five suggestions do not include history as a subject to be studied. In fact, I regard history as the single most important idea for our youth to take with them into the future. I call it an idea rather than a subject because every subject has a history, and its history is an integral part of the subject. History, we might say, is a meta-subject. No one can claim adequate knowledge of a subject unless one knows how such knowledge came to be. I would, of course, favor "history" courses (let us say, in American history), although I have always thought such courses ought to be called "histories" so that our youth would understand that what once happened has been seen from different points of view, by different people, each with a different story to tell.

My book is an example of this point. There is, in a sense, no such thing as "the Enlightenment." That is a name given at a later time by people who think something happened in the eighteenth century that hadn't happened before and influenced decisively the way people came to think and behave. I think so too. But Voltaire didn't. Neither did Hume or Kant or Jefferson. Each of them saw in their ideas continuities with prior ages, and they would be surprised at the special status we assign to their moment in time. No matter. Historians speak of the Enlightenment because they have a story to tell. And I have tried to use that story as an inspiration to confront an unknown future.

Of course, in a sense, there is no such thing as the twenty-first century, either. It is only a name, and we have no reason to suppose that how we have thought and behaved in the twentieth century need be, or will be, different because the Earth made another turn around the sun. But it is a name we use to foster hope, to inspire renewal, to get another chance to do it right. And it has seemed to me that if we try to remember how others before us tried to get it right, our own chances are improved.

As you know by now, I think those eighteenth-century fellows made a damn good try.

Appendix I

Letter from Lord Byron to Lord Holland, February 25, 1812

For my own part I consider the manufacturers as a much injured body of men, sacrificed to the views of certain individuals who have enriched themselves by those practices which have deprived the frame-workers of employment. For instance;—by the adoption of a certain kind of frame, one man performs the work of seven—six are thus thrown out of business. But it is to be observed that the work thus done is far inferior in quality, hardly marketable at home, and hurried over with a view to exportation. Surely, my Lord, however we may rejoice in any improvement in the arts which may be beneficial to mankind, we must not allow mankind to be sacrificed to improvements in mechanism. The maintenance and well-doing of the industrious poor is an object of greater consequence to the community than the enrichment of a few monopolists by any improvement in the implements of trade, which deprives the workman of his bread, and renders the labourer "unworthy of his hire."

My own motive for opposing the bill is founded on its palpable injustice, and its certain inefficacy. I have seen the state of these miserable men, and it is a disgrace to a civilized country. Their excesses may be condemned, but cannot be subject of wonder. The effect of the present bill would be to drive them into actual rebellion. The few words I shall venture to offer on Thursday will be founded upon these opinions formed from my own observations on the spot. By previous inquiry, I am convinced these men would have been restored to employment, and the country to tranquillity. It is, perhaps, not yet too late, and is surely worth the trial. It can never be too late to employ force in such circumstances. I believe your Lordship does not coincide with me entirely on this subject and most cheerfully and sincerely shall I submit to your superior judgement and experience, and take some other line of argument against the bill or be silent altogether, should you deem it more advisable. Condemning, as every one must condemn, the conduct of these wretches, I believe in the existence of grievances which call rather for pity than punishment.

From Lord Byron, *Selected Poems and Letters* (New York: New York University Press, 1977), pp. 448–49.

Appendix II

Comments on the Nature of Language by People Who Never Heard of Jacques Derrida

"The abuse of language occurs when its metaphorical nature is hidden, if the representation is *identified* with the thing represented. Therefore the linguistically hygienic use of metaphor depends on the full recognition of its limitations, that is, on critical consciousness of the generalizations, analogies, and abstractions involved."   —A. Rapoport, *Operational Philosophy*

"Since the concepts people live by are derived only from perceptions and from language and since the perceptions are received and interpreted only in light of earlier concepts, man comes pretty close to living in a house that language built."
                    —R. F. W. Smith, "Linguistics in
                              Theory and in Practice," *ETC.*

"The woof and warp of all thought and all research is symbols, and the life of thought and science is the life inherent in symbols; so that it is wrong to say that a good language is *important* to good thought, merely; for it is of the essence of it."
                    —C. S. Peirce, *Syllabus of Certain Topics of Logic*

"Naming selects, discriminates, identifies, locates, orders, arranges, systematizes. Such activities as these are attributed to 'thought' by older forms of expression, but they are much more properly attributed to language when language is seen as the living behavior of men."

—J. Dewey and A. F. Bentley, *Knowing and the Known*

"Language . . . does not permit the consideration of all aspects of behavior at once. An individual who wishes to speak or write about an event must use language which by necessity refers to some selected aspect of that event. A listener is capable of understanding the event in its entirety only after having studied not one but a great many selected aspects. Because this procedure is very time-consuming and renders written reports rather bulky, shortcuts are frequently taken and consequently many details are omitted. When fewer words are used and a lesser number of aspects are treated, the listener is inclined to pay too much attention to what is mentioned and disregard that which is omitted. This peculiarity of language and the resulting difficulties in the description of behavior have brought about certain verbal classifications which are not based upon the characteristics of pathology but rather upon those of the human reporter and the language he uses."   —J. Ruesch, *Disturbed Communication*

"The sorry fact is that our unconscious linguistic habits shape our religions and our philosophies, imprison our scientific statements about the world, are of the essence of the conflict of postulated culture with postulated culture, are involved with our wars and other human misunderstandings, and are a part even of our dreaming, our errors, and our neuroses."

—W. La Barre, *The Human Animal*

"Even on the verbal level, where they are most at home, educators have done a good deal less than they might reasonably have been expected to do in explaining to young people the nature, the limitations, the huge potentialities for evil as well as for good, of that greatest of all human inventions, language. Children should be taught that words are indispensable but also can be fatal—the only begetters of all civilization, all science, all consistency of high purpose, all angelic goodness, and the only begetters at the same time of all superstition, all collective madness and stupidity, all worse-than-bestial diabolism, all the dismal historical succession of crimes in the name of God, King, Nation, Party, Dogma."

—A. Huxley, "Education on the Nonverbal Level," *Daedalus*, Spring 1962

"Every language is a special way of looking at the world and interpreting experience.... One sees and hears what the grammatical system of one's language has made one sensitive to, has trained one to look for in experience. This bias is insidious because everyone is so unconscious of his native language as a system." —C. Kluckhohn, *Mirror for Man*

"Einstein pointed out that the statement 'Two events some distance apart occur simultaneously' cannot be used to derive any observable fact. Here was the impetus to a new philosophy whose chief preoccupation has been with the meaning of language. Since all knowledge must be set forth in language, it is the meaning we give to language which confers upon knowledge its weight and ambiguity.... What is curious is the fact that we look so seldom at the phenomenon of language, whose role in the world of affairs has no parallel."

—W. S. Beck, M.D., *Modern Science and the Nature of Life*

"We dissect nature along lines laid down by our native language. The categories and types that we isolate from the world of phenomena we do not find there because they stare every observer in the face; on the contrary, the world is presented in a kaleidoscopic flux of impressions which has to be organized by our minds—and this means largely by the linguistic system in our minds. We cut nature up, organize it into concepts, and ascribe significance as we do largely because we are parties to an agreement to organize it in this way—an agreement that holds throughout our speech community and is codified in the patterns of our language."

—B. L. Whorf, *Language, Thought, and Reality*,
ed. by J. B. Carroll

"The worker in the laboratory does not merely report and expound by the aid of analogy; that is how he thinks, also. The atom was once a hard little round particle, or later one with hooks on it. Recently it was a solar system. The classical dispute of physics about the nature of light was really asking, Is light like a shower of pebbles, or like ripples in a bathtub? The ultimate answer, Both, was one that was hard to accept. Why? Because it fitted into no preexisting conceptions; waves are waves, and pebbles are pebbles—there is nothing in common experience that has the properties of both."

—D. O. Hebb, *The Organization of Behavior*

"If a conceptual distinction is to be made . . . the machinery for making it ought to show itself in language. If a distinction cannot be made in language it cannot be made conceptually."

—N. R. Hanson, *Patterns of Discovery*

"When the mind is thinking, it is talking to itself."   —Plato

"Language, as such, is man's primary vehicle for thinking. Brains think with words. It is not mere verbal play to say that we cannot think without speaking, or speak without thinking. Most men suffer acute mental discomfort until the urge to express an idea, to define, to reason, to interpret has been formulated in words or in formulae, diagrams, equations or other symbolic devices which involve words. Without properly ordered specific words, thought is vague and misty, seen dimly through the depth of 'feeling' and 'intuition.'"

—J. O. Hertzler, *A Sociology of Language*

"Human beings do not live in the objective world alone, nor alone in the world of social activity as ordinarily understood, but are very much at the mercy of the particular language which has become the medium of expression for their society. It is quite an illusion to imagine that one adjusts to reality essentially without the use of language and that language is merely an incidental means of solving specific problems of communication and reflection. The fact of the matter is that the 'real world' is to a large extent unconsciously built up on the language habits of the group." —E. Sapir, *Culture, Language, and Personality*

"The purpose of Newspeak was not only to provide a medium of expression for the world-view and mental habits proper to the devotees of Ingsoc, but to make all other modes of thought impossible." —G. Orwell, *1984*

"There is a basic scheme of classification *built into* our common speech and language. This built-in classification system directs us so that we observe the things we can readily classify with the names we know, while we tend strongly to overlook or disregard everything else. We see with our categories." —W. Johnson, *Verbal Man*

181

"Before the intellectual work of conceiving and understanding of phenomena can set in, the work of *naming* must have preceded it, and have reached a certain point of elaboration. For it is this process which transforms the world of sense impression, which animals also possess, into a mental world, a world of ideas and meanings. All theoretical cognition takes its departure from a world already preformed by language; the scientist, the historian, even the philosopher, lives with his objects only as language presents them to him. This immediate dependence is harder to realize than anything that the mind creates mediately, by conscious thought processes." —E. Cassirer, *Language and Myth*

"We find the discoveries of modern science, or the utterances of modern writing, strange, but much of this strangeness is due to our provincialism concerning language—especially our own language. Insofar as we Westerners conceive of the universe as a collection of simple 'things' distinct in nature, yet taking part in 'actions,' we are certainly doing that universe an injustice." —M. Girsdansky, *The Adventure of Language*

"Words play their familiar tricks even with the thinking of the scientist, who may forget that in his necessary use of word symbols for his thinking and communication (space, time, IQ, attitude, etc.) he is employing abstractions which he cannot, as a scientist, implicitly or unconsciously assume as real in investigation. It is only to the extent that the investigator is aware of his own transformation of adjectival or adverbial relationships into noun qualities that he maintains the possibility of discovering new conditional relationships except for which a phenomenon would not exist." —F. P. Kilpatrick, *Explorations in Transactional Psychology*

"The denial that language is of the essence of thought, is not the assertion that thought is possible apart from the other activities coordinated with it. Such activities may be termed the expression of thought. When these activities satisfy certain conditions, they are termed a language."

—A. N. Whitehead, *Modes of Thought*

"Diagnosis is changing because we are changing our concepts of illness and disease. . . . But it is very difficult to rid our thinking and our language of the old entity concept of illness. We often speak in figurative terms of 'fighting the disease,' 'facing it,' of having a cancer, of suffering from arthritis, or of being afflicted with high blood pressure. This argot reflects the tendency to go on thinking of all diseases as a thing, a horrid, hateful, alien thing which invades the organism. . . .

"But one truth which has to be learned, and re-learned, and re-learned again, because we continually forget it, is that two apparently opposite things can be true. It is sometimes true that disease is an invasion; in other instances it is just as true that disease is not an invasion.

". . . Illness is in part what the world has done to a victim, but in a larger part it is what the victim has done with his world, and with himself." —K. Menninger, *The Vital Balance*

"The child is taught to accept 'tree' and not 'boojum' as the agreed sign for that (pointing to the) object. We have no difficulty in understanding that the word 'tree' is a matter of convention. What is much less obvious is that convention also governs the delineation of the thing to which the word is assigned. For the child has to be taught not only what words are to stand for what things, but also the way in which his culture has tacitly agreed to divide things from each other, to mark out the boundaries within our daily experience. Thus, scientific convention decides whether an eel shall be a fish or a snake, and grammatical convention determines what experiences shall be called objects and what shall be called events or actions."

—A. Watts, *The Way of Zen*

Appendix III

On the Origin of Childhood and Why It Is Disappearing

Childhood is a social artifact, not a biological category. Our genes contain no clear instructions about who is and who is not a child, and the laws of survival do not require that a distinction be made between the world of the adult and the world of the child. In fact, if we take the word "children" to mean a special class of people somewhere between the ages of seven and, say, seventeen, who require special forms of nurturing and protection, and who are believed to be qualitatively different from adults, then there is ample evidence that children have existed for less than four hundred years. Indeed, if we use the word "children" in the fullest sense in which the average North American understands it, childhood is not much more than two hundred years old. To take one small example: The custom of celebrating a child's birthday did not exist in America throughout most of the eighteenth century, and the precise marking of a child's age in any way is a relatively recent cultural tradition, no more than two hundred years old.

To take a more important example: As late as 1890, high schools in the United States enrolled only seven percent of the fourteen- through seventeen-year-old population. Along with many younger children, the other ninety-three percent worked at adult labor, some of them from sunup to sunset in all of our great cities.

185

But it would be a mistake to confuse social facts with social ideas. The *idea* of childhood is one of the great inventions of the Renaissance, perhaps its most humane one. Along with science, the nation-state, and religious freedom, childhood as both a social principle and a psychological condition emerged around the seventeenth century. Up until that time, children as young as six and seven simply were not regarded as fundamentally different from adults. The language of children, their way of dressing, their games, their labor, and their legal rights were the same as adults'.

It was recognized, of course, that children tended to be smaller than adults, but this fact did not confer upon them any special status; there certainly did not exist any special institutions for the nurturing of children. Prior to the seventeenth century, for example, there were no books on childrearing or, indeed, any books about women in their role as mothers. Children were always included in funeral processions, there being no reason anyone could think of to shield them from death. Neither did it occur to anyone to keep a picture of a child, whether that child lived to adulthood or had died in infancy. Nor are there any references to children's speech or jargon prior to the seventeenth century, after which they are found in abundance. If you have ever seen thirteenth- or fourteenth-century paintings of children, you will have noticed that they are always depicted as small adults. Such paintings are entirely accurate representations of the psychological and social perceptions of children prior to the seventeenth century. Here is how the historian J. H. Plumb puts it: "There was no separate world of childhood. Children shared the same games with adults, the same toys, the same fairy stories. They lived their lives together, never apart. The coarse village festivals depicted by Breughel, showing men and women besotted with drink, groping for each other with unbridled lust, have children eating and drinking with the adults. Even in the soberer pictures of wedding feasts and dances, the children are enjoying themselves alongside their elders, doing the same things."

In *A Distant Mirror,* Barbara Tuchman's marvelous book about the fourteenth century, she summed it up this way: "If children survived to age seven, their recognized life began, more or less as miniature adults. Childhood was already over." Now why this was the case is fairly complicated to say. For one thing, as Tuchman indicates, most children did not survive; their mortality rate was extraordinarily high, and it is not until the late fourteenth century that children are even mentioned in wills and testaments—an indication that adults did not expect them to be around very long. Certainly, adults did not have the emotional commitment to children that we accept as normal. Then, too, children were regarded primarily as economic utilities, adults being less interested in the character and intelligence of children than in their capacity for work. But I believe the primary reason for the absence of the idea of childhood is to be found in the communication environment of the medieval world; that is to say, since most people did not know how to read or did not need to know how to read, a child became an adult—a fully participating adult—at the point where he or she learned how to speak. Since all important social transactions involved face-to-face oral communication, full competence to speak and hear—which is usually achieved by age seven—was the dividing line between infancy and adulthood. That is why the Catholic Church designated age seven as the age at which a person can know the difference between right and wrong, the age of reason. That is why children were hanged, along with adults, for stealing or murder. And that is why there was no such thing as elementary education in the Middle Ages, for where biology determines communication competence there is no need for such education. There was no intervening stage between infancy and adulthood because none was needed—until the middle of the fifteenth century.

At that point an extraordinary event occurred that not only changed the religious, economic, and political face of Europe but eventually created our modern idea of childhood. I am referring, of course, to the invention of the printing press. Of course, no one had the slightest idea in 1450 that the printing press would have such powerful effects on our society as it did. When Gutenberg announced that he could manufacture books, as he put it, "without the help of reed, stylus, or pen but by wondrous agreement, proportion, and harmony of punches and types," he did not imagine that his invention would undermine the authority of the Catholic Church. And yet, less than eighty years later, Martin Luther was, in effect, claiming that with the word of God available in every home, Christians did not require the papacy to interpret it for them. Nor did Gutenberg have any idea that his invention would create a new class of people—namely, children.

To get some idea of what reading meant in the two centuries following Gutenberg's invention, consider the case of two men— one by the name of William, the other by the name of Paul. In the year 1605, they attempted to burglarize the house of the Earl of Sussex. They were caught and convicted. Here are the exact words of their sentences as given by the presiding magistrate: "The said William does not read, to be hanged. The said Paul reads, to be scarred." Paul's punishment was not exactly merciful; it meant he would have to endure the scarring of his thumbs. But Paul survived because he had pleaded what was called "benefit of clergy," which meant that he could meet the challenge of reading at least one sentence from an English version of the Bible. And *that* ability alone, according to English law in the seventeenth century, was sufficient grounds to exempt him from the gallows. I suspect the reader will agree with me when I say that of all the suggestions about how to motivate people to learn to read, none can match the method of seventeenth-century England. As a matter of fact, of the 203 men convicted of hangable crimes in Norwich in the year 1644, about half of them pleaded "benefit of clergy," which suggests that the English were able to produce, at the very least, the most literate population of felons in history.

But of course that was not the only thing produced. As I implied, childhood was an outgrowth of literacy. And it happened because in less than one hundred years after the invention of the printing press, European culture became a reading culture; which is to say, adulthood was redefined. One could not become an adult unless one knew how to read. To experience God, one had to be able, obviously, to read the Bible. To experience literature, one had to be able to read novels and personal essays, forms of literature that were wholly created by the printing press. Our earliest novelists—for example, Richardson and Defoe—were themselves printers, and Sir Thomas More worked hand in hand with a printer to produce what may be called our first science-fiction novel—his *Utopia*. Of course, to learn science, one had to know how to read, but by the beginning of the seventeenth century, one could read science in the vernacular—that is, in one's own language. Sir Francis Bacon's *The Advancement of Learning*, published in 1605, was the first scientific tract an Englishman could read in English. Alongside all of this, Europeans rediscovered what Plato had known about learning to read—that it is best done at an early age. Since reading is, among other things, an unconscious reflex as well as an act of recognition, the habit of reading must be formed in that period when the brain is still engaged in the task of acquiring oral language. The adult who learns to read after his or her oral vocabulary is completed rarely if ever becomes a fluent reader.

What this came to mean in the seventeenth century is that the young had to be separated from the rest of the community to be taught how to read; that is, to be taught how to function as adults. Before the printing press, children became adults by learning to *speak*, for which all people are biologically programmed. After the printing press, children had to *earn* adulthood by achieving literacy, for which people are not biologically programmed. This meant that schools had to be created. In the Middle Ages, there was no such thing as primary education. In England, for example, there were thirty-four schools in the entire country in the year 1480. By the year 1660, there were more than 450, one school for every twelve square miles. With the establishment of schools, it was inevitable that the young would come to be viewed as a special class of people whose minds and character were qualitatively different from adults'. Because the school was designed for the preparation of literate adults, the young came to be perceived not as miniature adults but as something quite different—unformed adults. School learning became identified with the special nature of childhood. Childhood, in turn, became defined by school attendance, and the word "schoolboy" became a synonym for the word "child."

We began, in short, to see human development as a series of stages, in which childhood is a bridge between infancy and adulthood. For the past three hundred years, we have been developing and refining our concept of childhood; we have been developing and refining institutions for the nurturing of children; and we have conferred upon children a preferred status, reflected in the special ways we expect them to think, talk, dress, play, and learn.

All of this, I believe, is now coming to an end, at least in the United States. And it is coming to an end because our communication environment has been radically altered once again, this time by electronic media, especially television. Television has a transforming power at least equal to that of the printing press and possibly as great as that of the alphabet itself. And it is my contention that with the assistance of other media such as radio, film, and records, television has the power to lead us to childhood's end.

Here is how the transformation is happening. To begin with, television is essentially nonlinguistic; it presents information mostly in visual images. Although human speech is heard on television, and sometimes assumes importance, people mostly watch television. And what they watch are rapidly changing visual images—as many as 1,200 different shots every hour. The average length of a shot on network television is 3.5 seconds; the average for a commercial is 2.5 seconds. This requires very little analytic decoding. In America, television watching is almost wholly a matter of pattern recognition. What I am saying is that the *symbolic form* of television does not require any special instruction or learning. In America, television-viewing begins at about the age of eighteen months, and by thirty-six months children begin to understand and respond to television imagery. They have favorite characters, they sing jingles they hear, and they ask for products they see advertised. There is no need for any preparation or prerequisite training for watching television; it needs no analogue to the McGuffey *Reader*. Watching television requires no skills and develops no skills. That is why there is no such thing as remedial television-watching. That is also why you are no better today at watching television than you were five years ago, or ten. And that is also why there is no such thing, in reality, as children's programming.

Everything is for everybody. So far as symbolic form is concerned, *ER* is as sophisticated or as simple to grasp as *Sesame Street*. Unlike books, which vary greatly in syntactical and lexical complexity and which may be scaled according to the ability of the reader, television presents information in a form that is undifferentiated in its accessibility. And that is why adults and children tend to watch the same programs.

To summarize, television erases the dividing line between childhood and adulthood in two ways: It requires no instruction to grasp its form, and it does not segregate its audience. Therefore, it communicates the same information to everyone, simultaneously, regardless of age, sex, level of education, or previous condition of servitude.

One might say that the main difference between an adult and a child is that the adult knows about certain facets of life—its mysteries, its contradictions, its violence, its tragedies—that are not considered suitable for children to know. As children move toward adulthood, we reveal these secrets to them in ways we believe they are prepared to manage. That is why there is such a thing as children's literature. But television makes this arrangement quite impossible. Because television operates virtually around the clock, it requires a constant supply of novel and interesting information to hold its audience. This means that all adult secrets—social, sexual, physical, and the like—are revealed. Television forces the entire culture to come out of the closet, taps every existing taboo. Incest, corruption, sadism—each is now merely a theme for one or another television show. And, of course, in the process, each loses its role as an exclusively adult secret.

As a consequence of all this, childhood innocence is impossible to sustain, which is why children have disappeared from television. Indeed, all the children on television shows are depicted as merely small adults, in the manner of thirteenth- and fourteenth-century paintings. On any of the soap operas or family shows or situation comedies you will see children whose language, dress, sexuality, and interests are not different from those of the adults on the same shows.

And yet, as television begins to render invisible the traditional concept of childhood, it would not be quite accurate to say that it immerses us in an adult world. Rather, it uses the material of the adult world as the basis for projecting a new kind of person altogether. We might call this person the adult-child. For reasons that have partly to do with the accessibility of its symbolic form, and partly to do with its commercial base, television promotes as desirable many of the attitudes that we associate with childishness—for example, an obsessive need for immediate gratification, a lack of concern for consequences, an almost promiscuous preoccupation with consumption. Television seems to favor a population that consists of three age groups: on the one end, infancy; on the other, senility; and in between, a group of indeterminate age, where everyone is psychologically somewhere between twenty and thirty and remains that way until dotage descends.

In short, our culture is providing fewer reasons and opportunities for childhood. I am not so single-minded as to think that television alone is responsible for this transformation. The decline of the family, the loss of a sense of roots—forty million Americans change residence every year—and the elimination, through technology, of much significance in adult work are other factors. But I believe television creates a communication context that encourages the idea that childhood is neither desirable nor necessary; indeed, that we do not need children.

Notes

Chapter One: A Bridge to the 18th Century

1. Berlin, 1956, p. 29.

Chapter Two: Progress

1. Gay, p. 245.
2. Redman, pp. 109–10.
3. See *The Jefferson Bible*.
4. Paine, p. 50.
5. Brinton, p. 295.
6. Durant, p. 231.
7. Im Hof, p. 8.
8. Cassirer, p. 6.
9. Brinton, p. 262.
10. Redman, p. 77.
11. Bury, p. 5.
12. Crocker, p. 194.
13. See Johnson, pp. 1–27.
14. Bauman, p. 17.

Chapter Three: Technology

1. Lasch, 1991, p. 41.
2. Negroponte, pp. 145–46.

3. See Oppenheimer's article in *The Atlantic*, July 1997.
4. Marx, p. 150.

Chapter Four: Language

1. The term "the Enlightenment" (with a definite article) is an English mistranslation of the German *"Aufklärung,"* meaning simply "enlightenment." Moreover, *the* Enlightenment is not possible to translate into French, the standard term being *"lumières,"* meaning "lights."
2. Berlin, 1956, p. 180.
3. Paine, p. 11.
4. Paine, p. 52.
5. Einstein, 1972, p. 2.
6. Paine, p. 69.
7. Gergen, p. 119.
8. Cited in Hayek, p. 201.
9. Cited in Julius, p. 189.
10. The *London Times*, September 30, 1997.

Chapter Five: Information

1. Hart, p. 8.
2. Hart, p. 8.
3. Hart, p. 15.
4. Mumford, p. 136.
5. Wilson, p. 140.

Chapter Six: Narratives

1. See Thomas L. Haskell, "Talk in the Age of Interpretation," *The Journal of American History*, p. 1003.
2. Commager, 1977, p. 237.
3. Russell, 1961, p. 45.

4. Einstein, 1954, p. 40.
5. Lerner, 1961, p. 424.
6. Einstein, 1954, p. 42.
7. Lerner, 1961, p. 424.
8. Havel, *Prognosis* 16, No. 3, August 6, 1993, p. 4.
9. Both quotes are found in James Reston, Jr., *Galileo: A Life*, New York: HarperCollins, pp. 136 and 142.

Chapter Seven: Children

1. Stone, p. 258.
2. Stone, p. 257.
3. Dewey, 1899, p. 55.
4. I refer to Channel 1, which is a daily ten-minute news program accompanied by two minutes of commercial advertising interspersed among the news programming. Channel 1 is broadcast daily to more than 350,000 middle and high schools nationwide.

Chapter Eight: Democracy

1. Tocqueville, p. 189.
2. Tocqueville, p. 473.
3. Tocqueville, p. 58.
4. Tocqueville, pp. 5–6.
5. Tocqueville, p. 260.
6. Dewey, 1899, p. 157.
7. Commager, 1977, p. 188.
8. Commager, 1977, p. 194.
9. Molinaro, p. 335.
10. Tocqueville, p. 506.
11. Eisenstein, p. 119.
12. I refer here to the famous article by David Putnam, "Bowling Alone." Putnam discovered that, while more people are bowling today, they tend to bowl alone and not as part of a team or a league.

Chapter Nine: Education

1. Green, p. 41.
2. Commager, 1977, p. 125.

Bibliography

Adamson, J. W., ed. *Froebel's Chief Writings on Education*. Translated by S. S. F. Fletcher and J. Welton. London: Edward Arnold & Co., 1912.

Anderson, Walter Truett, ed. *The Truth About the Truth: De-confusing and Reconstructing the Postmodern World*. New York: Putnam, 1995.

Appleby, Joyce, et al., eds. *Knowledge and Postmodernism in Historical Perspective*. New York: Routledge, 1996.

Bauman, Zygmunt. *Modernity and the Holocaust*. Ithaca, N.Y.: Cornell University Press, 1989.

Behar, Joseph E., ed. *Mapping Cyberspace: Social Research on the Electronic Frontier*. Oakdale, N.Y.: Dowling College Press, 1997.

Berlin, Isaiah. *Concepts and Categories: Philosophical Essays*. Edited by Henry Hardy. New York: Penguin Books, 1981.

———, ed. *The Age of Enlightenment: The Eighteenth Century Philosophers*. New York: Signet Classics, 1956.

Brinton, Clarence Crane. *Ideas and Men: The Story of Western Thought*. Englewood Cliffs, N.J.: Prentice-Hall, 1963.

Bronowski, Jacob. *The Origins of Knowledge and Imagination*. New Haven: Yale University Press, 1978.

Buchholz, Ester Schaler. *The Call of Solitude: Alonetime in a World of Attachment*. New York: Simon & Schuster, 1997.

Bury, J. B. *The Idea of Progress: An Inquiry into Its Origin and Growth*. New York: Dover Publications, 1987.

Butt, John. *The Augustan Age*. London: Hutchinson House, 1950.

Cassirer, Ernst. *The Philosophy of the Enlightenment*. Translated by Fritz C. A. Koelln and James P. Pettegrove. Princeton: Princeton University Press, 1951.

Commager, Henry Steele. *The Empire of Reason: How Europe Imagined and*

Bibliography

America Realized the Enlightenment. New York: Anchor Press/Doubleday, 1977.

————, ed. *Living Ideas in America.* New York: Harper and Bros., 1951.

Compayré, Gabriel. *Pestalozzi and Elementary Education.* Translated by R. P. Jago. New York: Thomas Y. Crowell & Co., 1907.

Crocker, Lester G., ed. *The Age of Enlightenment.* New York: Harper & Row, 1969.

Crone, Brinton. *A History of Western Morals.* New York: Paragon House, 1990.

Delbanco, Andrew. *The Death of Satan: How Americans Have Lost the Sense of Evil.* New York: Farrar, Straus and Giroux, 1995.

Derrida, Jacques. *Speech and Phenomena: And Other Essays on Husserl's Theory of Signs.* Translated by David B. Allison. Evanston, Ill.: Northwestern University Press, 1973.

Dewey, John. *Freedom and Culture.* New York: Capricorn Books, 1963.

————. *The School and Society.* Chicago: University of Chicago Press, 1899.

Durant, Will. *The Story of Philosophy.* New York: Washington Square Press, 1961.

Einstein, Albert. *Ideas and Opinions.* Arenel, N.J.: Wings Books, 1954.

————. *The Meaning of Relativity.* Princeton: Princeton University Press, 1972.

Eisenstein, Elizabeth. *The Printing Press as an Agent of Change.* New York: Cambridge University Press, 1979.

Fowler, Bridget. *Pierre Bourdieu and Cultural Theory: Critical Investigations.* London: Sage Publications, 1997.

Franklin, Benjamin. *The Autobiography of Benjamin Franklin & Selections from His Writings.* Introduction by Henry Steele Commager. New York: A. S. Barnes & Co., Inc., 1944.

Freud, Sigmund. *The Future of an Illusion.* Translated and edited by James Strachey. New York: W. W. Norton & Co., 1961.

Gay, Peter. *The Enlightenment: An Interpretation—The Rise of Modern Paganism.* New York: W. W. Norton & Co., 1966.

Gergen, Kenneth J. *The Saturated Self: Dilemmas of Identity in Contemporary Life.* New York: Basic Books, 1991.

Gould, Stephen Jay. *Full House: The Spread of Excellence from Plato to Darwin.* New York: Three Rivers Press, 1996.

Bibliography

Green, J. A. *Life and Work of Pestalozzi*. Baltimore: Warwick & York, Inc., University Tutorial Press [1912?].

Hart, James D. *The Popular Book: A History of America's Literary Taste*. New York: Oxford University Press, 1950.

Hayek, F. H. *The Counter-Revolution of Science: Studies on the Abuse of Reason*. Indianapolis: Liberty Press, 1952.

Hays, Mary. *Appeal to the Men of Great Britain in Behalf of Women*. Series edited by Gina Luria. New York: Garland Publishing, Inc., 1974.

Horkheimer, Max, and Theodor Adorno. *Dialectic of Enlightenment*. New York: Continuum, 1972.

Hume, David. *An Inquiry Concerning the Principles of Morals*. New York: Liberal Arts Press, 1957.

Im Hof, Ulrich. *The Enlightenment: An Historical Introduction*. Translated from the German by William E. Yuill. Oxford; Cambridge: Blackwell Publishers, 1994.

Jefferson, Thomas. *The Jefferson Bible: The Life and Morals of Jesus of Nazareth*. Boston: Beacon Press, 1989.

Johnson, Paul. *Intellectuals*. New York: Harper & Row, 1988.

Julius, Anthony. *T. S. Eliot, Anti-Semitism, and Literary Form*. Cambridge: Cambridge University Press, 1995.

Lasch, Christopher. *The Revolt of the Elites and the Betrayal of Democracy*. New York: W. W. Norton & Co., 1996.

———. *The True and Only Heaven: Progress and Its Critics*. New York: W. W. Norton & Co., 1991.

Lemert, Charles. *Social Things: An Introduction to the Sociological Life*. Lanham, Md.: Rowman & Littlefield Publishers, 1997.

Lerner, Max. *America as a Civilization: Life and Thought in the United States Today*. New York: Simon & Schuster, 1957.

———. *The Essential Works of John Stuart Mill*. New York: Bantam Books, 1961.

Lewis, C. S. *The Abolition of Man*. New York: Touchstone/Simon & Schuster, 1996.

Lyotard, Jean-François. *The Postmodern Condition: A Report on Knowledge*. Translated by Geoff Bennington and Brian Massumi. Minneapolis: University of Minnesota Press, 1993.

Manguel, Alberto. *A History of Reading*. New York: Viking, 1996.

Marx, Karl, and Friedrich Engels. *The German Ideology*. New York: International Publishers, 1972.

201

Mehlman, Jeffrey. *Cataract: A Study in Diderot.* Middletown, Conn.: Wesleyan University Press, 1979.

Molinaro, Matie, Corinne McLuhan, and William Toye, eds. *Letters of Marshall McLuhan.* New York: Oxford University Press, 1987.

Mumford, Lewis. *Technics and Civilization.* New York: Harcourt, Brace & World, 1934.

Negroponte, Nicholas. *Being Digital.* New York: Vintage, 1996.

Nisbet, Robert. *History of the Idea of Progress.* New York: Basic Books, 1980.

Noble, David F. *Progress Without People: In Defense of Luddism.* Chicago: Charles H. Kerr Publishing Co., 1993.

———. *The Religion of Technology: The Divinity of Man and the Spirit of Invention.* New York: Alfred A. Knopf, 1997.

Overy, Richard. *Why the Allies Won.* New York: W. W. Norton & Co., 1996.

Paine, Thomas. *The Age of Reason.* New York: First Carol Publishing Group, 1991.

Perkinson, Henry. *How Things Got Better: Speech, Writing, Printing, and Cultural Change.* Westport, Conn.: Bergin & Garvey, 1995.

Postman, Neil. *Amusing Ourselves to Death: Public Discourse in the Age of Show Business.* New York: Viking, 1985.

———. *Conscientious Objections: Stirring Up Trouble About Language, Technology, and Education.* New York: Alfred A. Knopf, 1988.

———. *The End of Education: Redefining the Value of School.* New York: Alfred A. Knopf, 1996.

———. *Technopoly: The Surrender of Culture to Technology.* New York: Vintage, 1993.

———. and Charles Weingartner. *Teaching as a Subversive Activity.* New York: Delta/Dell, 1969.

Pucci, Suzanne L. *Diderot and a Poetics of Science.* New York: Peter Lang, 1986.

Rahman, Mohammed Mujeeb. *The Betrayal of Intellect in Higher Education.* Toronto: OmniView Publishing, 1997.

Redman, Ben Ray, ed. *The Portable Voltaire.* New York: Penguin, 1949.

Roszak, Theodore. *The Cult of Information: A Neo-Luddite Treatise on High Tech, Artificial Intelligence, and the True Art of Thinking.* Berkeley and Los Angeles: University of California Press, 1994.

Rousseau, Jean-Jacques. *Reveries of the Solitary Walker.* Translated by Peter France. London: Penguin Books, 1979.

Bibliography

Russell, Bertrand. *Mysticism and Logic.* New York: Anchor Press/Doubleday, 1961.

———. *The Scientific Outlook.* New York: W. W. Norton & Co., 1962.

Sambrook, James. *The Eighteenth Century: The Intellectual and Cultural Context of English Literature, 1700–1789.* London: Longman, 1986.

Sarup, Madan. *An Introductory Guide to Post-structuralism and Postmodernism.* Athens: University of Georgia Press, 1989.

Shelley, Percy Bysshe. *Shelley's Defence of Poetry and Blunden's Lectures on "Defence."* Darby, Pa.: Darby Books, 1969.

Sherman, Carol. *Diderot and the Art of Dialogue.* Geneva: Librairie Droz, 1976.

Snyder, Louis L. *The Age of Reason.* New York: D. Van Nostrand Company, 1955.

Sale, Kirkpatrick. *Rebels Against the Future.* New York: Addison-Wesley, 1995.

Stone, Lawrence. *The Family, Sex and Marriage in England 1500–1800* (abridged edition). New York: Harper Torchbooks, 1979.

Teich, Albert, ed. *Technology and the Future.* New York: St. Martin's Press, 1997.

Tocqueville, Alexis de. *Democracy in America.* Translated by George Lawrence. New York: Doubleday, 1969.

West, Thomas G. *Vindicating the Founders: Race, Sex, Class, and Justice in the Origins of America.* Lanham, Md.: Rowman & Littlefield Publishers, 1997.

Wilson, Arthur M. *Diderot.* New York: Oxford University Press, 1972.

Acknowledgments

Without the assistance of Ruth Liberman I could not have completed this book. I am indebted to her for her patience and intelligence. I should also like to thank William Phillips for his assistance. I am indebted, as well, to my colleagues in the Department of Culture and Communication at New York University, whose conversations have helped me to think through some of the problems I have tried to confront in this book.

Index

Index

children, 116–35
  as economic creatures, 125–6, 187
  education of, 30, 33, 37, 118–22,
    131–3, 155–7, 187, 190
  Freud's conception of, 123
  labor by, 19, 126, 133
  protection of, 33–4, 118
  socialization of, 124–5, 133, 157
  television and, 49, 52, 59, 85, 124,
    132, 135, 188–9
  working women and, 130
Christianity, 114, 188
  idea of progress in, 26–7
  rationalism and, 22–3, 30
  See also Bible
Clinton, Bill, 134, 135
clocks, mechanical, 48–9, 152, 168
cloning, 12–13, 16, 95
Coleridge, Samuel Taylor, 31
Commager, H. S., 103, 104
communism, 112
community, 53, 151, 153
computers, 13, 37, 39–40, 46–8, 55, 90,
    97, 132, 170, 171
Comte, Auguste, 63
Condillac, E. B. de, 25, 60
Condorcet, Marquis de, 29, 73, 80
Cooper, James Fenimore, 68
Copley, J. S., 117
creation science, 167–70
crimes, children's, 133, 187
critical thinking, 160–2
Cutler, Manasseh, 104

D'Alembert, Jean, 60, 73
Darwinian evolution, 25, 34, 39, 102,
    108, 114, 167–8
Debray, Régis, 80
Declaration of Independence, 19, 23, 67,
    105, 107, 138, 153
deconstruction, 8, 10, 78–9
deduction, 62–3
Defoe, Daniel, 18, 60, 64, 189
Deists, 22, 104
de Man, Paul, 79

democracy, 77, 90, 136–54
  invention of, 15
  participatory, 53–4, 146–7, 150
  printing and, 142–5, 148–52
denial, 7–8
Derrida, Jacques, 58, 69, 76, 78–80,
    177
Descartes, René, 27, 76
devil, belief in, 7–8, 10
Dewey, John, 71, 123–4, 160, 178
"Dial-a-Story," 128
Diderot, Denis, 17, 23, 40, 42, 58, 60,
    64, 73, 80, 103, 138, 147
  Encyclopédie of, 25, 30, 86
Disney, Walt, 50
distance learning, 54
Dole, Robert, 52
doorknobs, talking to, 41–5
Dyson, Esther, 51

Eddington, Arthur, 69
Edison, Thomas Alva, 50
education, 155–74
  of children, 30, 33, 37, 118–22, 131–3,
    155–7, 187, 190
  in Colonies, 84–5
  in comparative religion, 171–3
  computers in, 46–8
  in 18th century, 83
  as national resource, 157–9
  for skepticism, 159–62
  technology, 170–1
Edwards, Jonathan, 104
egoism, 151, 152
Einstein, Albert, 69–71, 110–11
Eisenstein, Elizabeth, 149, 151, 162
electronic town hall meeting, 54, 147
Eliot, T. S., 8–9, 10
Emerson, Ralph Waldo, 37
Encyclopédie, 25, 30, 86
Enlightenment, 3, 7, 23, 39, 40, 50, 100,
    110, 112, 138, 157, 159, 160
  American, 105–6
  idea of progress in, 26–7, 32–5
  language in, 58–68, 72–81

208

Index

Index

Index

Milton, John, 59
Minsky, Marvin, 13
Molière, 69
Monroe, James, 66
Montaigne, Michel de, 59
Montesquieu, Baron de, 28, 30, 60, 138, 141, 147
Montessori, Maria, 120, 132
More, Thomas, 189
Morris, William, 35, 36
Morse, Samuel, 50
Moses, 102
Muhammad, 11–12, 102
Mumford, Lewis, 17, 40, 85, 88, 152
Mussolini, Benito, 139
myths, *see* narratives

narratives, 9–10, 101–15
in democracy, 148, 153–4
natural law, 107, 110, 111
natural philosophers, 61
natural science
expository prose of, 61
narrative provided by, 109
rationalism and, 24–9
Nazism, 112, 113
Negroponte, N., 37, 41–2
Neill, A. S., 120, 156
newspapers, 59, 82, 87, 90–8, 142–3
Newton, Isaac, 18, 25, 27, 61, 63, 103, 114, 168
Nietzsche, Friedrich, 14, 40, 41, 100–1, 103, 106
Northwest Ordinance, 67, 104
novels, 59–60

Ong, Walter, 149
Orwell, George, 169, 181
Owen, Robert, 38

Paine, Thomas, 17, 19, 22, 24, 29, 42, 60, 77, 103–5, 107, 158
prose of, 64–6, 73–4
pamphlets, 142–3
Peirce, C. S., 71, 177
Penn, William, 60

Pestalozzi, Johann, 17, 33, 37, 120, 156–7
philosophers and philosophes, 103–11
Piaget, Jean, 120, 127
Plato, 15, 72, 79, 136, 139, 180, 189
Plumb, J. H., 186
Plutarch, 159
Poe, Edgar Allan, 142
poetry, 31–2, 52
Pope, Alexander, 29, 83
postmodernism, 8, 101, 109
language in, 8, 14, 58, 69–81
texts in, 78–81
poststructuralism, 68–9
Priestley, Joseph, 29, 61, 63, 104, 158, 162
printing, 49, 52, 59, 85, 124, 132, 135, 188–9
in democracy, 142–52
progress, 23, 25–35, 104, 108
technological, 36–42
20th-century disbelief in, 40–1
propaganda, 164
prose, 59–68, 144
Protestant conception of childhood, 121, 122

question-asking, 161–2, 164, 167

Rapoport, Anatole, 71, 177
rationalism, 21–35, 100–1
print and, 149–51
reading, 148–52, 188–90
Reagan, Ronald, 28, 51
reality
language and, 69–74
photography and, 88
"social construction" of, 74–5, 78
"rearview mirror" thinking, 5
relativity, 70
religion
freedom of, 20, 33, 105, 107, 108
rejection of, 22, 64, 66, 100
study in schools of, 171–3
Reynolds, Joshua, 18, 117
rhetoric, 15, 163

211

Index

Index

A NOTE ABOUT THE AUTHOR

Neil Postman is University Professor, Paulette Goddard Chair of Media Ecology, and Chair of the Department of Culture and Communication at New York University. Among his twenty books are studies of childhood (*The Disappearance of Childhood*), public discourse (*Amusing Ourselves to Death*), education (*Teaching as a Subversive Activity*), and the impact of technology (*Technopoly*).

A NOTE ABOUT THE TYPE

This book was set in Janson, a typeface thought to have been made by the Dutchman Anton Janson, who was a practicing type-founder in Leipzig during the years 1668–1687. However, it has been conclusively demonstrated that these types are actually the work of Nicholas Kis (1650–1702), a Hungarian, who most probably learned his trade from the master Dutch typefounder Dirk Voskens. The type is an excellent example of the influential and sturdy Dutch types that prevailed in England up to the time William Caslon (1692–1766) developed his own incomparable designs from them.

Composed by NK Graphics,
Keene, New Hampshire
Printed and bound by R. R. Donnelley & Sons,
Harrisonburg, Virginia
Designed by Soonyoung Kwon